RASPBERRY PI PICO W STEP-BY-STEP USER GUIDE FOR QUICK SETUP

RUTH WEALTH

Table of Contents

INTRODUCTION

The Raspberry Pi Pico W is the first small wireless board made specifically for physical computing; it's the successor to the popular Pico board. It's built around the in-house ARM chip RP2040 created by The Raspberry Foundation. Both boards are built around the same material as the original Pico board, which we discussed earlier. The Bluetooth connectivity on the new Pico W model is significantly improved over previous models. The Infineon CYW43439 wireless chip comes with an IEEE 802.11 b/g/n wireless LAN chip, and Wi-Fi connectivity is also included.

The Raspberry Pi Pico W is identical to the original Pico board in every way except for the fact that it has 40 pins. The Pico W has 30 GPIOs accessible through its header; however, only 26 of them are multipurpose. The remaining two pins are GP23, GP24, GP25, and GP29.

Since these four pins are not exposed on the header, we only have access to 26 functional GPIOs with the Pico W board. PicoW supports a 3-Pin Header near the RP2040 Chip that is used for debug purposes. All GPIO pins on the board operate at 3.3V and have no other additional headers or options.

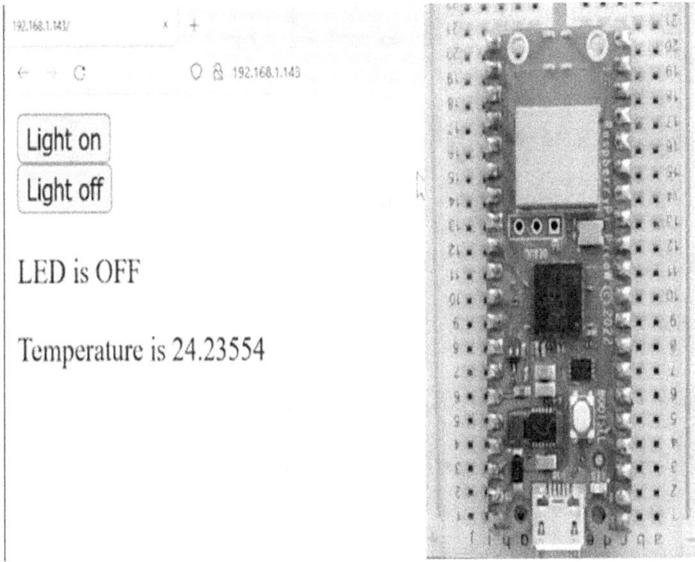

WiFi devices allow computers to easily communicate with each other and the internet. This led to the internet of things (IoT) revolution thanks to technology.

Chapter One

Connect your Raspberry Pi Pico W to a wifi hub.

Create a web server on your Raspberry Pi Pico W to display a webpage.

By using your website, you can also monitor the temperature data gathered by the onboard LED on the Pico W Raspberry Pi.

In order to create this item, you need the following:

A micro USB data cable and Raspberry Pi Pico W are required to use this application.

A computer connected to your network is required for this software to work.

Thonny Python includes an IDE called the Thonny Python API.

Add Thonny to a Raspberry Pi for storage.

Thonny needs to be updated to the latest version on Raspberry Pi OS.

It's possible to open a terminal window by clicking on the icon in the top-left corner of the screen or pressing Ctrl+Alt+T simultaneously.

Update OS and Thonny by typing this in the window.

Update software packages via the apt command using upgrade or update flags. Then use yaourt to reinstall them.

Thonny can be installed on other operating systems.

You can install the latest Thonny IDE or update an existing one on Windows, macOS and Linux.

Go to thonny.org using a web browser.

At the top-right corner of the browser window, you'll see links to download macOS and Windows operating systems. Additionally, you'll find instructions on how to use Linux.

Install Thonny by downloading the necessary files and running them.

Opening Thonny

Open Thonny from your application launcher by accessing it through your operating system's program list. Click on the file name to access it.

Type the following code into the Thonny program window and then press the Run button. After this, you'll be prompted to name the file; choose a name and then press OK to save it.

```python
print('Hello World!')
```

Change the theme and font in Thonny to a different option.

Thonny's themes and fonts can be easily manipulated. This includes changing the text color, background image or size. By using Thonny, users can customize the software to match their specific needs.

To Change the theme and font:

Open the Tools menu and select Options.

Look in the "Theme & Font" section of the menu.

Click each drop-down menu to choose the best settings for your needs.

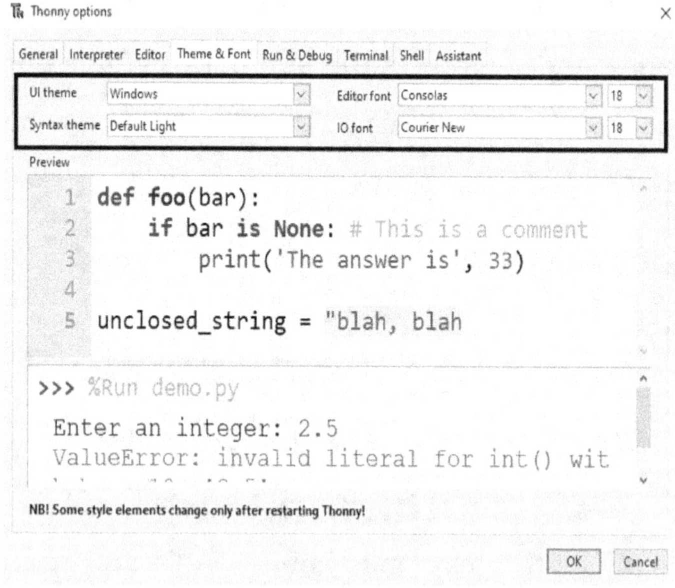

When finished, press OK.

Avoid using handwriting fonts due to their illegibility. Additionally, avoid using overly complex or dirty fonts for the same reason

Chapter Two

Setting up your Raspberry Pi Pico W

The Raspberry Pi Pico W can be connected to a MicroPython-enabled Raspberry Pi.

Using MicroPython, you can write code to interact with electronics devices using your knowledge of Python. This is possible because the language runs on microcontrollers such as the Raspberry Pi Pico W.

Plug the small end of the micro USB cable into the Pico W board.

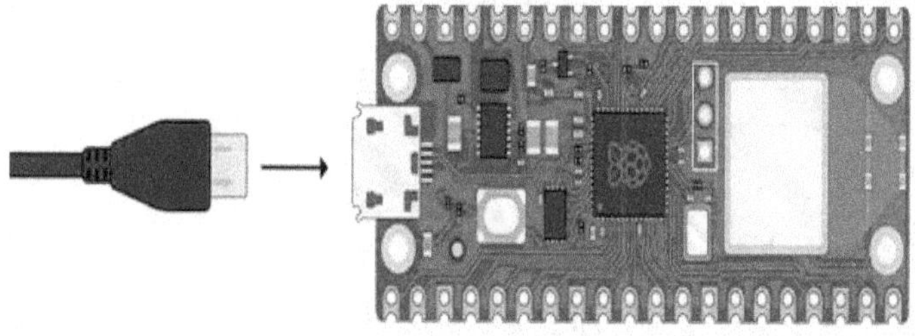

As soon as you press the BOOTSEL button on your Raspberry Pi Pico W, hold down the button.

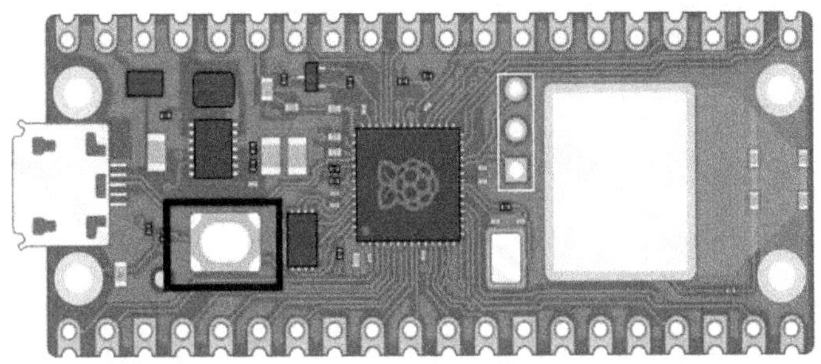

This cord connects your Raspberry Pi, laptop or desktop computer to the other end.

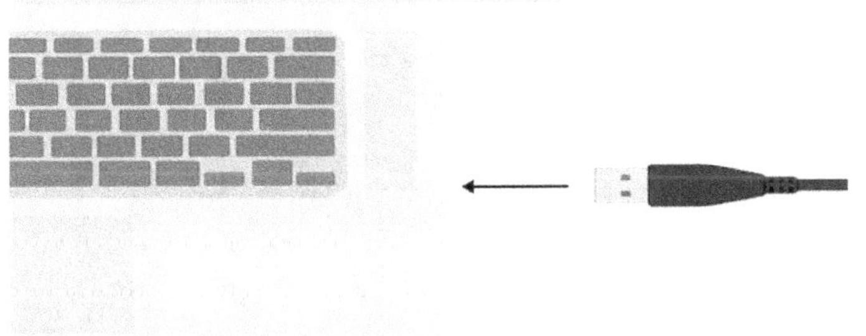

You need to download firmware into your file manager's folder: drop the file into the folder when your Pico opens. It must then close when you finish. You can also do this via connecting to Raspberry Pi Pico via USB.

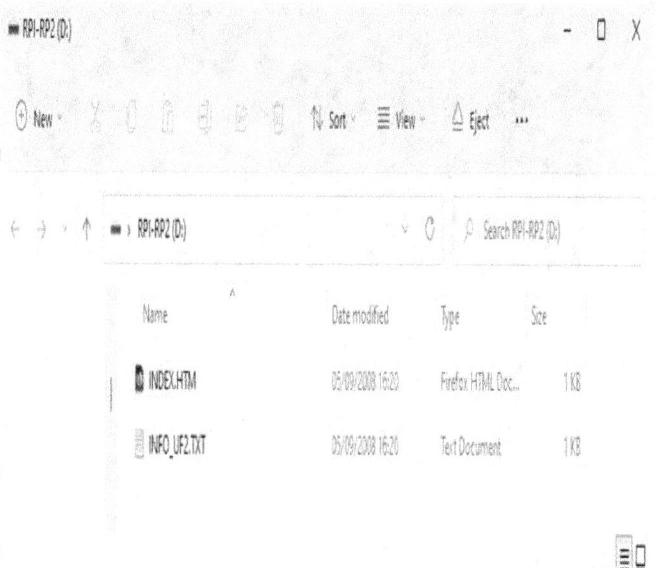

Open the Thonny editor by opening its file.

The text in the bottom right corner of the Thonny Python editor notes which version of the language is being used.

In order to select the correct version of MicroPython for the Raspberry Pi Pico, click on the text that says 'MicroPython (Raspberry Pi Pico).' Then choose the option labeled 'MicroPython (Raspberry Pi Pico).'

The same interpreter which runs Thonny (default)
Alternative Python 3 interpreter or virtual environment
MicroPython (Raspberry Pi Pico)
MicroPython (ESP32)
MicroPython (ESP8266)
CircuitPython (generic)

Configure interpreter...

Python 3.7.9

I'm unable to connect to the Pico because I don't know if the firmware is installed.

You can access the interpreters by clicking the box in the bottom right corner of your Thonny window. Once you click it, a pop-up menu appears with options. Click one and connect your Raspberry Pi Pico W via a micro USB cable.

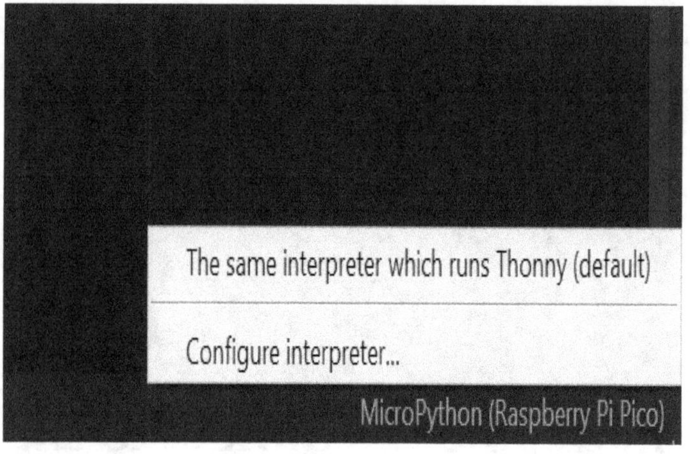

You need to physically connect your Raspberry Pi Pico W while holding down the BOOTSEL button in order to display it in the list. From there, you must follow the instructions above to reinstall the firmware on your device. Alternatively, you can use a program to do this for you. Any version of Pico won't display if you don't see it in the list though.

My Pico still can't connect to the firmware installed on its device.

As a beginner-friendly alternative to MicroPython, the picozero library for Raspberry Pi Pico is useful to new users.

You need to install the picozero library as a Thonny package to complete projects in this route.

From the Tools menu in Thonny, choose Manage Packages to access a list of installed applications.

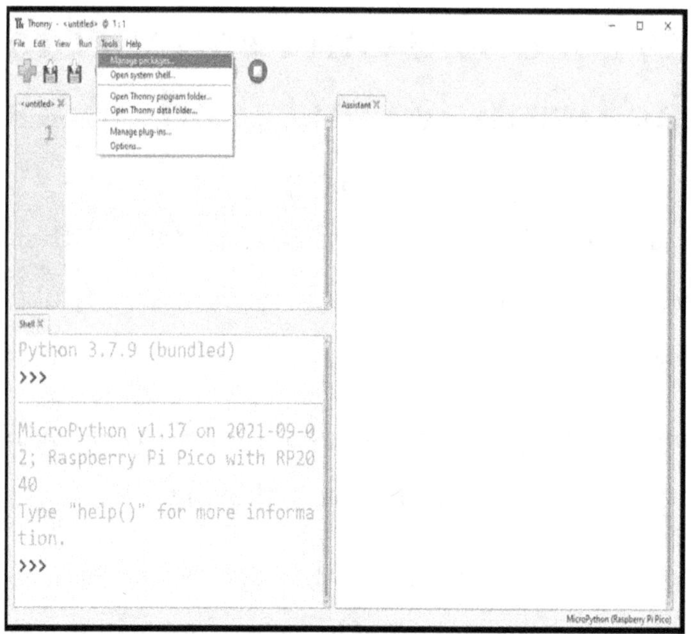

When searching for packages on PyPi in the window titled "Manage Raspberry Pi Pico Packages," type picozero and click the Search button.

Tap on install.

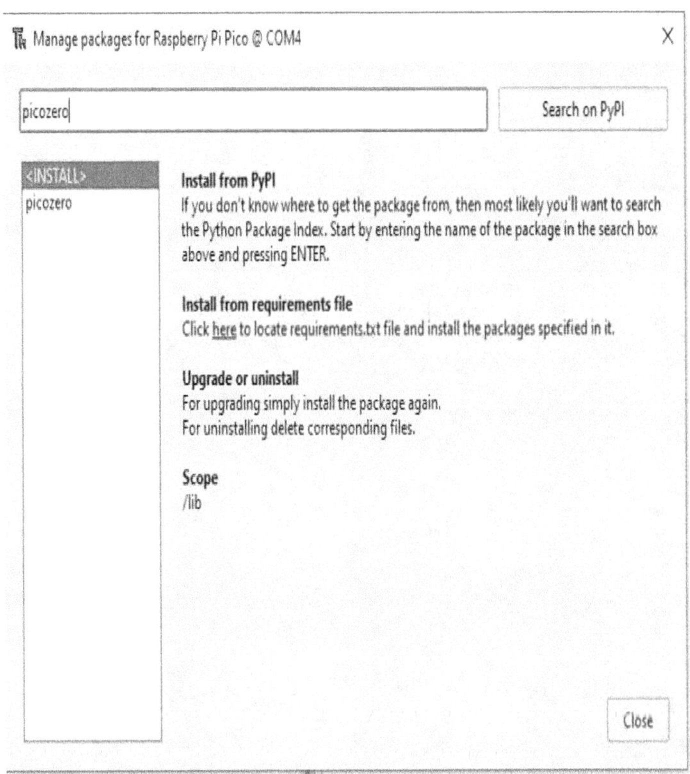

Find Picozero in the search results by clicking on it.

Go ahead and install the program.

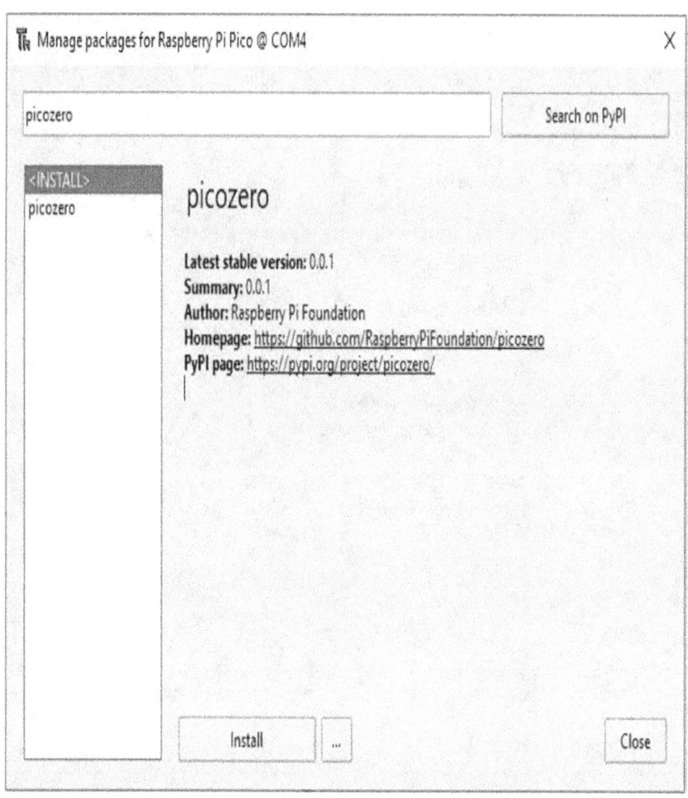

After the program is installed, close the window when finished. Then quit and restart Thonny.

Download the picozero library file from the website and place it on your Raspberry Pi Pico W for easier library installation.

Chapter Three

Creating an offline picozero program.

Even without internet connectivity or administrative rights to install packages with Thonny, you can still use the picozero library with your Raspberry Pi Pico.

You can download a specific file to a USB flash drive by connecting another computer to the internet.

1. Go to the picozero.py file in the picozero GitHub repository using a web browser.

2. After viewing the picozero page, right-click and choose "Save Page as" from the menu.

3. The file name must remain unchanged when choosing a location to download the program. This can be done by selecting a location and keeping the chosen filename picozero.py.

Using the Thonny file manager, transfer files.

4. To connect the Pico to the computer, plug a micro USB cable into it.

5. Select the Files option from the View menu after loading Thonny through your app's menu.

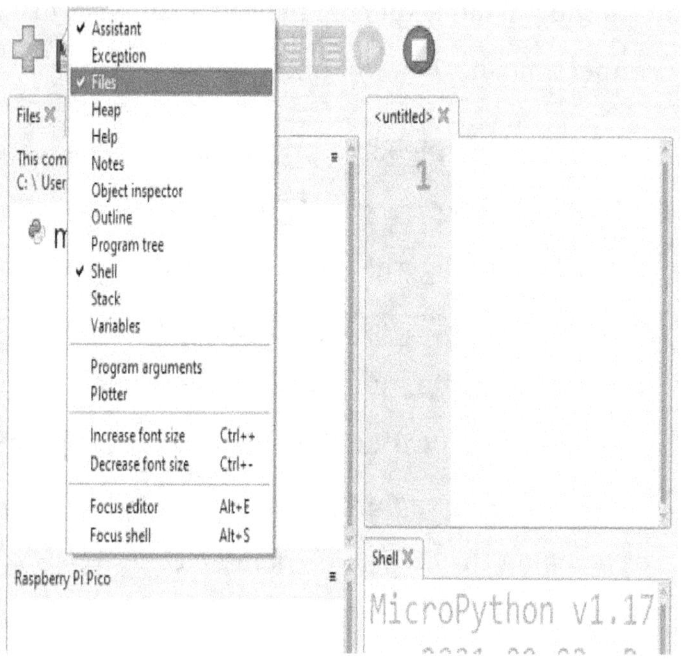

1. In order to access the .py file saved in the picozero directory, use the directed path.

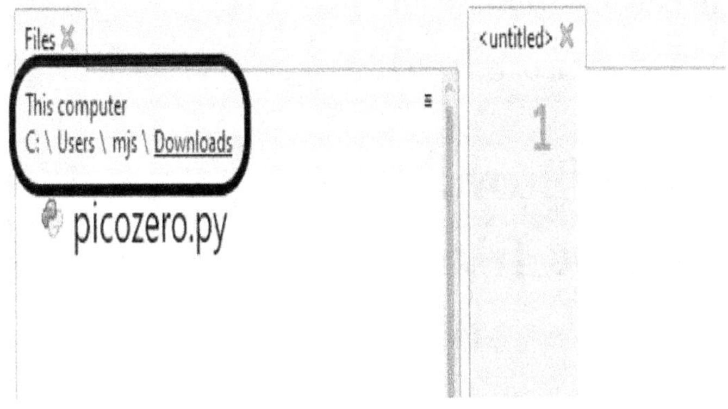

1. Open picozero.py by right-clicking it and selecting Upload from the menu.

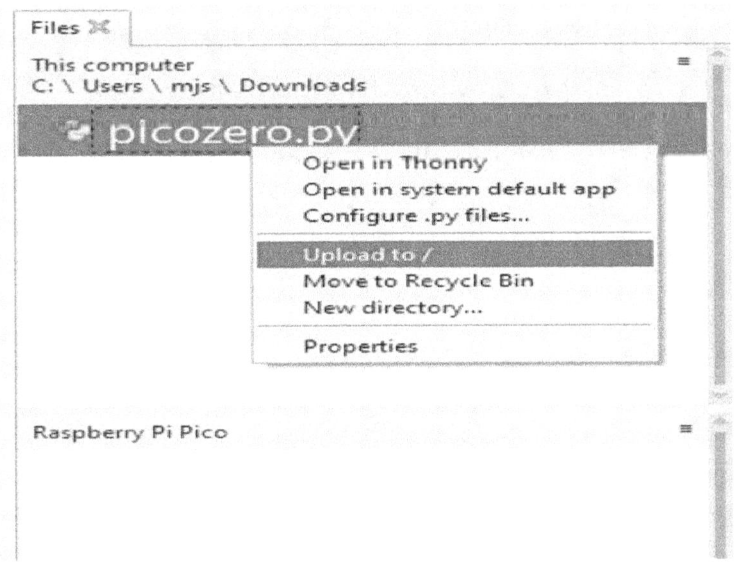

1 The new picozero.py library should be available to view on the Raspberry Pi Pico.

Use Thonny to copy and paste a file into its proper location.

1. To copy text from the picozero.py file into another program, open it in a separate window and use the keyboard's Ctrl button along with A for all the text.

2. Press Ctrl+V to paste the contents of picozero.py into Thonny's untitled tab.

3. To save any file, press Ctrl + s and choose to save the file to the Pico Raspberry Pi.

1. Click OK to name the file picozero.py.

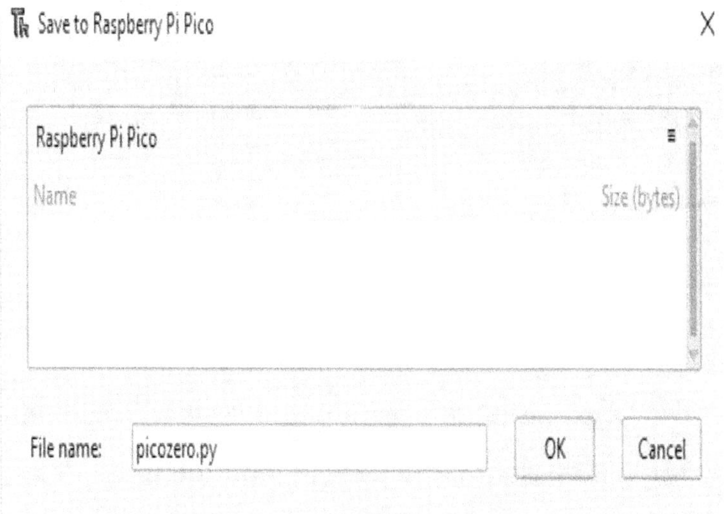

Connect your Raspberry Pi model Pico W to a Wifi network.

Using the MicroPython programming language, you can connect your Raspberry Pi Pico W to a WLAN, or WiFi network, without being connected to the internet. This is called "WLAN hacking."

```
Shell

MicroPython v1.18-659-g7a6d6452f-dirty on 2022-06-15; Raspberry Pi Pico W with RP2040
Type "help()" for more information.
>>> %Run -c $EDITOR_CONTENT

Waiting for connection...
Waiting for connection...
Waiting for connection...
Connected on 192.168.1.143

>>>
```

Keep your passwords private and secure. You'll add your WiFi password to your Python file in this step. Don't share your file with anyone you wouldn't want to tell your password to; otherwise, someone will be able to access your file.

To connect to a wireless internet network, you need to know the name of the network's set identifier, or SSID. Your WiFi password can be found written on your wireless router or you can change the default one to something unique. You also need to have the password when setting up your camera.

Thonny needs access to a WiFi network to import the packages needed to interact with it. Additionally, Thonny reads the onboard temperature sensor and illuminates the onboard LED.

```
1   import network
2   import socket
3   from time import sleep
4   from picozero import pico_temp_sensor, pico_led
5   import machine
```

Select This Computer when prompted to save this code.

To complete this step, obtain the SSID and password to your network from your Pi Pico W's onboard LED. Additionally, connect the board to an LED light source.

```
7   ssid = 'NAME OF YOUR WIFI NETWORK'
8   password = 'YOUR SECRET PASSWORD'
```

Start building a mechanism that connects to your wireless network by creating a wlan object, turning on its wireless capability, and inputting your network name and password.

```
12    def connect():
13        #Connect to WLAN
14        wlan = network.WLAN(network.STA_IF)
15        wlan.active(True)
16        wlan.connect(ssid, password)
```

When connecting to a wireless network, your device will send and receive data; in other words, it won't instantly connect to the network. Instead, it'll establish a connection with the router by exchanging handshakes. This process can be automated by creating a loop in Python that continuously sends and receives requests.

```python
12  def connect():
13      #Connect to WLAN
14      wlan = network.WLAN(network.STA_IF)
15      wlan.active(True)
16      wlan.connect(ssid, password)
17      while wlan.isconnected() == False:
18          print('Waiting for connection...')
19          sleep(1)
```

Test your WLAN settings after printing them out. You'll need to call your function when testing. When using the Raspberry Pi Pico W's wireless connection, always ensure that the bottom lines of your script are all functional commands. This ensures that any code you add afterward won't reset the device when it stops running.

```python
12  def connect():
13      #Connect to WLAN
14      wlan = network.WLAN(network.STA_IF)
15      wlan.active(True)
16      wlan.connect(ssid, password)
17      while wlan.isconnected() == False:
18          print('Waiting for connection...')
19          sleep(1)
20      print(wlan.ifconfig())
21
22  try:
23      connect()
24  except KeyboardInterrupt:
25      machine.reset()
```

Look for this result when running your code in test: saving and running it. Your test should show you different IP addresses than the original.

```
Waiting for connection...
Waiting for connection...
Waiting for connection...
Waiting for connection...
Waiting for connection...
('192.168.1.143', '255.255.255.0', '192.168.1.254', '192.168.1.254')
```

The Raspberry Pi Pico W has difficulty connecting

To configure your Raspberry Pi Pico W, only need the information provided by the wlan.ifconfig() function. One piece of this information is the IP address of the Raspberry Pi Pico W, which you can retrieve from the first line of the function's output. By prefixing a string with an f, a variable's address can be printed when it's enclosed in braces.

```
12   def connect():
13       #Connect to WLAN
14       wlan = network.WLAN(network.STA_IF)
15       wlan.active(True)
16       wlan.connect(ssid, password)
17       while wlan.isconnected() == False:
18           print('Waiting for connection...')
19           sleep(1)
20       ip = wlan.ifconfig()[0]
21       print(f'Connected on {ip}')
22
23
24   try:
25       connect()
26   except KeyboardInterrupt:
27       machine.reset()
```

You can return the value of the Raspberry Pi Pico W's IP address when your function is called. This value can then be stored when your function is called again.

```python
12  def connect():
13      #Connect to WLAN
14      wlan = network.WLAN(network.STA_IF)
15      wlan.active(True)
16      wlan.connect(ssid, password)
17      while wlan.isconnected() == False:
18          print('Waiting for connection...')
19          sleep(1)
20      ip = wlan.ifconfig()[0]
21      print(f'Connected on {ip}')
22      return ip
23
24
25  try:
26      ip = connect()
27  except KeyboardInterrupt:
28      machine.reset()
```

Next, backup your project.

Open a socket.

You connect to your wireless network to open a socket in this step.

```
>>> %Run -c $EDITOR_CONTENT
 Waiting for connection...
 Waiting for connection...
 Waiting for connection...
 Connected on 192.168.1.143
 <socket state=1 timeout=-1 incoming=0 off=0>
```

A server running on Raspberry Pi Foundation servers hosts the website you are currently viewing. This is how a server can listen for a client that wants to connect. A Raspberry Pi Pico W connected to the internet via an open socket serves as the server. When a web browser on another computer attempts to connect, its contents are instantly transferred to the client.

When connecting to a service via a socket, you need to provide the port number and an IP address for the piece of software. This is how computers tell where to send requests for data. When setting up a web server, port 80 is normally used. This is because port 80 is typically used for web servers. Many games in Stardew Valley use port 24642 when playing with other players; it's also the port that web servers connect to.

Create a new function that can be used to open a socket. Name it Above Your Try/Except, or AYATE, and put it above your try/except. Next, assign the socket an IP address and port number.

```
25    def open_socket(ip):
26          # Open a socket
27          address = (ip, 80)
28
29
30    try:
31          connect()
32    except KeyboardInterrupt:
33          machine.reset()
```

After creating your socket, publish a function that listens on port 80. Don't forget to implement this portion of your code.

```python
25    def open_socket(ip):
26        # Open a socket
27        address = (ip, 80)
28        connection = socket.socket()
29        connection.bind(address)
30        connection.listen(1)
31        print(connection)
32
33    try:
34        ip = connect()
35        open_socket(ip)
36    except KeyboardInterrupt:
37        machine.reset()
```

This is the result of running your code: something similar to this.

```
>>> %Run -c $EDITOR_CONTENT
Waiting for connection...
Waiting for connection...
Waiting for connection...
Waiting for connection...
Waiting for connection...
Connected on 192.168.1.143
<socket state=1 timeout=-1 incoming=0 off=0>
```

Although your socket still has an error indicated by state=1, it is functioning properly.

When done, swap the current print with a replacement. Then maintain the replacement as a separate variable.

```python
25  def open_socket(ip):
26      # Open a socket
27      address = (ip, 80)
28      connection = socket.socket()
29      connection.bind(address)
30      connection.listen(1)
31      return connection
32
33
34  try:
35      ip = connect()
36      connection = open_socket(ip)
37  except KeyboardInterrupt:
38      machine.reset()
```

Your Raspberry Pi Pico W listens for incoming connection requests on port 8o. Once a connection is established, the device starts serving HTML code to a connected web browser. Therefore, your project can be saved before continuing with the next steps.

Chapter Four

Create a website page.

You need to create a webpage that your Raspberry Pi Pico W web server can send to a client web browser. You'll first test this webpage on your computer before creating it. Then, you'll add the code to your Python script so that your Raspberry Pi Pico W can serve the webpage. You need to do this next step so you can test the webpage on your computer again. Then, you can add your script to your web server and start serving the webpage.

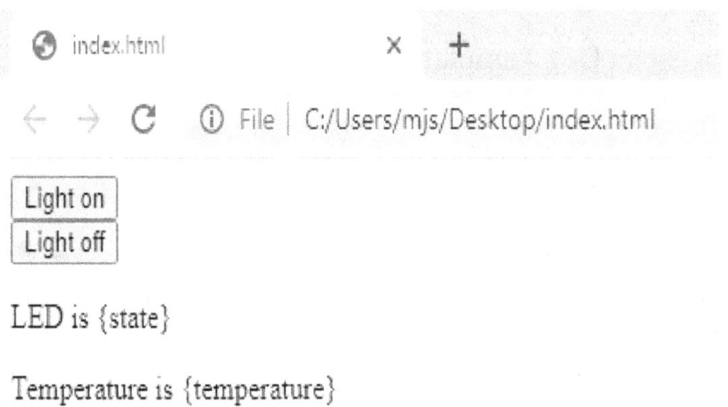

To create a webpage, you only need a text editor, such as VSCode, TextEdit or Notepad. However, Thonny doesn't support writing HTML. Instead, it can be used to create websites that web browsers interpret and offer some interactivity. An easy way to make a webpage with Thonny is by simply adding text to the document.

Out of the box, Thonny displays index.html as its first page. You can name this file whatever you choose, but the standard is to name it index.html . Add the .html file extension when sharing a file via any method; if using Thonny, save on This Computer.

A basic HTML template is required to begin with.

```
1   <!DOCTYPE html>
2   <html>
3   <body>
4   </body>
5   </html>
```

You can use a button to toggle the onboard LED light on or off.

```html
1  <!DOCTYPE html>
2  <html>
3  <body>
4  <form action="./lighton">
5  <input type="submit" value="Light on" />
6  </form>
7  </body>
8  </html>
```

After saving your file, locate it in your file manager. Click the file to open it in your default web browser; Google Chrome is used in the example below. Additionally, you should select File > Save As to save a copy of your file in its original location.

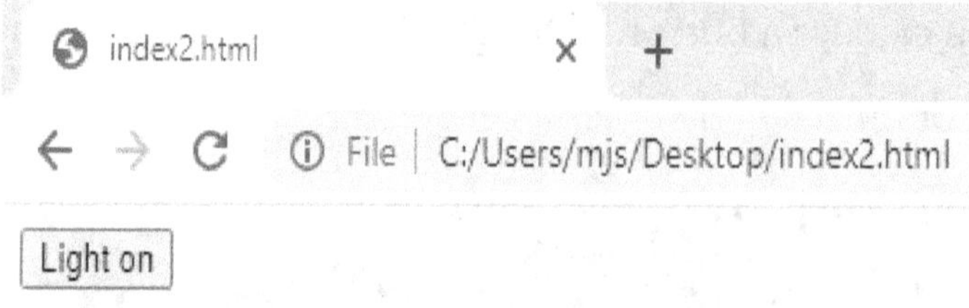

Plus a 3rd button to turn the LED light off.

```
1   <!DOCTYPE html>
2   <html>
3   <body>
4   <form action="./lighton">
5   <input type="submit" value="Light on" />
6   </form>
7   <form action="./lightoff">
8   <input type="submit" value="Light off" />
9   </form>
10  </body>
11  </html>
```

Additional information can be added to the end of the page, such as the temperature and status of the Raspberry Pi Pico W LED.

```
1   <!DOCTYPE html>
2   <html>
3   <body>
4   <form action="./lighton">
5   <input type="submit" value="Light on" />
6   </form>
7   <form action="./lightoff">
8   <input type="submit" value="Light off" />
9   </form>
10  <p>LED is {state}</p>
11  <p>Temperature is {temperature}</p>
12  </body>
13  </html>
```

Your website should have a layout similar to this.

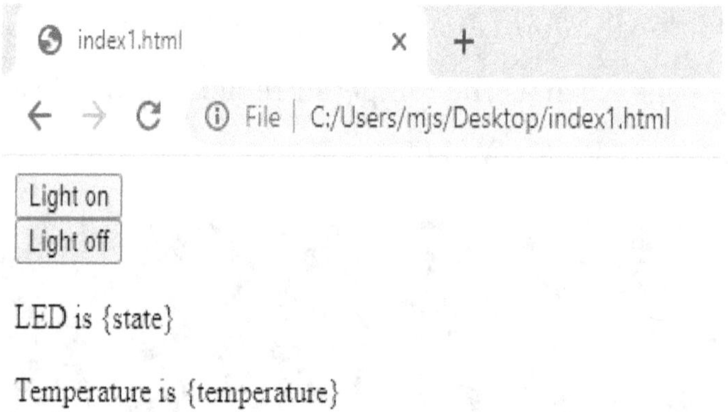

In order to incorporate this code into your script, switch back to your original Python file in Thonny. Adding this code into your file allows you to create a working webpage.

Create a new function called webpage with two parameters— temperature and state.

```
34    def webpage(temperature, state):
35        #Template HTML
```

fstrings allow you to conveniently insert placeholders for temperature and state into your strings. You can currently only use this function on HTML text that you've already written and tested.

```
34    def webpage(temperature, state):
35        #Template HTML
36        html = f"""
37                <!DOCTYPE html>
38                <html>
39                <form action="./lighton">
40                <input type="submit" value="Light on" />
41                </form>
42                <form action="./lightoff">
43                <input type="submit" value="Light off" />
44                </form>
45                <p>LED is {state}</p>
46                <p>Temperature is {temperature}</p>
47                </body>
48                </html>
49                """
```

You can return any HTML string from your function.

```python
34    def webpage(temperature, state):
35        #Template HTML
36        html = f"""
37                <!DOCTYPE html>
38                <html>
39                <form action="./lighton">
40                <input type="submit" value="Light on" />
41                </form>
42                <form action="./lightoff">
43                <input type="submit" value="Light off" />
44                </form>
45                <p>LED is {state}</p>
46                <p>Temperature is {temperature}</p>
47                </body>
48                </html>
49                """
50        return str(html)
```

Save your project before continuing.

You need to update your program first before you can test this code. That's because it's not supporting HTML yet; that change comes next.

Any devices connected to the WiFi on your network can access your website. This is different from other websites stored on remote servers; only computers connected to your WiFi are able to view and interact with your website. Creating a website isn't difficult, and there are many examples on this site. For more information, see some of our other projects on HTML coding. There are also many tutorials on creating your own websites!

Serve your website.

You need to start up your web server so a client can connect to it and control its LED as well as the temperature.

Before starting your web server, you must create a function that uses the Connection object as a parameter. This object stores the state and temperature variables, which you must set for your HTML data. State should be set to OFF when the server is started, and the LED should be turned off to ensure proper functionality.

```
53    def serve(connection):
54        #Start a web server
55        state = 'OFF'
56        pico_led.off()
57        temperature = 0
```

Your Raspberry Pi Pico W needs to be connected to the internet when your web browser requests a connection. Once you connect, the data you send must be split into 1024-sized chunks. Your browser needs to inform you of the specific request it's making. Is it requesting a blank page or a non-existent page?

When maintaining web hosting, it's important to keep the server online and listening for connections at all times. This can be accomplished by including a loop that continually executes the command True. Before processing any requests, add the lines of code shown below to your program. Then use print() to view the request's contents. Next, call the serve function from your bottom section of code.

```python
53  def serve(connection):
54      #Start a web server
55      state = 'OFF'
56      pico_led.off()
57      temperature = 0
58      while True:
59          client = connection.accept()[0]
60          request = client.recv(1024)
61          request = str(request)
62          print(request)
63          client.close()
64
65
66  try:
67      ip = connect()
68      connection = open_socket(ip)
69      serve(connection)
70  except KeyboardInterrupt:
71      machine.reset()
```

In a web browser, enter the program's IP address into a blank box in the form of a hyperlink.

This message should appear in Thonny's output when viewed in its entirety.

```
>>> %Run -c $EDITOR_CONTENT
Waiting for connection...
Waiting for connection...
Waiting for connection...
Connected on 192.168.1.143
b'GET / HTTP/1.1\r\nHost: 192.168.1.143\r\nUser-Agent: Mozilla/5.0 (Windows NT 1
b'GET /favicon.ico HTTP/1.1\r\nHost: 192.168.1.143\r\nUser-Agent: Mozilla/5.0 (W
```

After creating a web page in a client browser, the
client requires the HTML code you wrote for next
steps.

```python
53    def serve(connection):
54        #Start a web server
55        state = 'OFF'
56        pico_led.off()
57        temperature = 0
58        while True:
59            client = connection.accept()[0]
60            request = client.recv(1024)
61            request = str(request)
62            print(request)
63            html = webpage(temperature, state)
64            client.send(html)
65            client.close()
```

```
66
67
68    try:
69        ip = connect()
70        connection = open_socket(ip)
71        serve(connection)
72    except KeyboardInterrupt:
73        machine.reset()
```

Thonny requires that you observe two separate output types when running the code. Click on any of the buttons displayed when running the code to refresh your page.

```
b'GET /lighton? HTTP/1.1\r\nHost: 192.168.1.143\r\nUser-Agent: Mozilla
```

and

```
b'GET /lightoff? HTTP/1.1\r\nHost: 192.168.1.143\r\nUser-Agent: Mozill
```

Check your options to see whether you have lighton or lightoff. The onboard LED on the Pico W can be controlled by using the requests.

It's best to handle being unable to split the request string into two parts in a try/except block. After that, fetch the first item in the list.

Switching the LED on lights the first item in a split. If the LED is switched off, you can turn off the LED.

```python
def serve(connection):
    #Start a web server
    state = 'OFF'
    pico_led.off()
    temperature = 0
    while True:
        client = connection.accept()[0]
        request = client.recv(1024)
        request = str(request)
        try:
            request = request.split()[1]
        except IndexError:
            pass
        if request == '/lighton?':
            pico_led.on()
        elif request =='/lightoff?':
            pico_led.off()
        html = webpage(temperature, state)
        client.send(html)
        client.close()
```

You need to run your code again once you refresh your browser window and press the buttons. When switched on, the onboard LED should blink while off when you press any of the buttons.

LEDs can be configured to display a specific message when used.

```python
53  def serve(connection):
54      #Start a web server
55      state = 'OFF'
56      pico_led.off()
57      temperature = 0
58      while True:
59          client = connection.accept()[0]
60          request = client.recv(1024)
61          request = str(request)
62          try:
63              request = request.split()[1]
64          except IndexError:
65              pass
66          if request == '/lighton?':
67              pico_led.on()
68              state = 'ON'
69          elif request =='/lightoff?':
70              pico_led.off()
```

```
71              state = 'OFF'
72          temperature = pico_temp_sensor.temp
73          html = webpage(temperature, state)
74          client.send(html)
75          client.close()
```

When you run the code, the text on the LED's current state should also appear on the web page when it's reloaded.

On-board temperature sensors provide a ballpark figure for how hot the CPU is. This can be used to display the temperature on a webpage.

You can check the temperature of the Raspberry Pi Pico W by covering one hand with another over it. Then, observe the temperature by refreshing a web page on your computer.

Microsoft Azure IoT Hub can be connected to the Raspberry Pi Pico W using MQTT and MicroPython.

Chapter Five

What is MQTT?

MQTT is short for Message Queue Telemetry Transport. It's one of the most popular protocols used for IoT projects due to its lightweight nature.

A Publish-Subscribe protocol called MQTT uses subjects to post data collected by Devices. These messages are then received by Subscribers through the use of topics.

What are Microsoft Azure IoT Hubs?

The Microsoft Azure IoT Hub service provides a connection point between millions of devices and other Azure services. It sits beyond the edge of Azure, making it accessible by millions of devices. The IoT Hub registers each device that connects to it. Each device's credentials are stored in a Registry.

Construct the Circuit steeply.

It's time to build a circuit once you have your Raspberry Pi Pico W set up.

To send messages from the IoT Hub, we'll connect a resistor and LED to our Pico W. When we press the button, we'll receive data from the LED and write it to our message.

To construct this circuit, you need to build a line with these components.

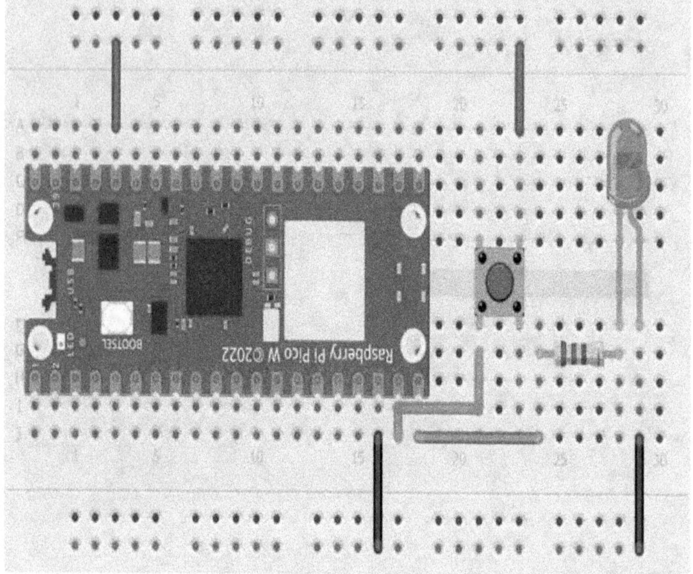

The Azure IoT Hub Circuit provides connectivity to the Raspberry Pi Pico W.

We connect a push-button to Pin 14 and an LED to Pin 15.

Creating an Azure IoT Hub is the next step after creating an Azure Machine Hub.

You need an Azure subscription to complete this tutorial. You can get a free trial here.

Since we're using the Free Tier of the Azure IoT Hub, this project will cost us absolutely nothing.

On the Azure Portal, click the "+ Create a Resource" button once you have your Azure Subscription properly configured.

Azure Portal adds a Resource Button to the My Portal area.

Search for "IoT Hub" by entering "IoT Hub" into the search box.

The Search Box on Azure Portal features a blue background.

In the Marketplace, click the IoT Hub item.

 The Azure Portal houses the Marketplace results for the IoT Hub.

Click the record button after choosing that option.

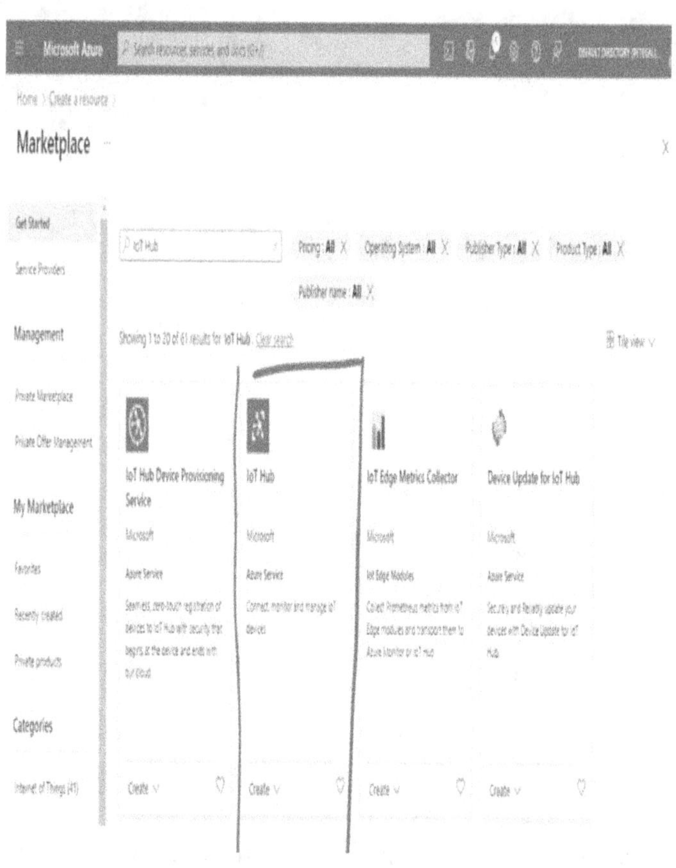

The Azure Portal features an IoT Hub Create Button.

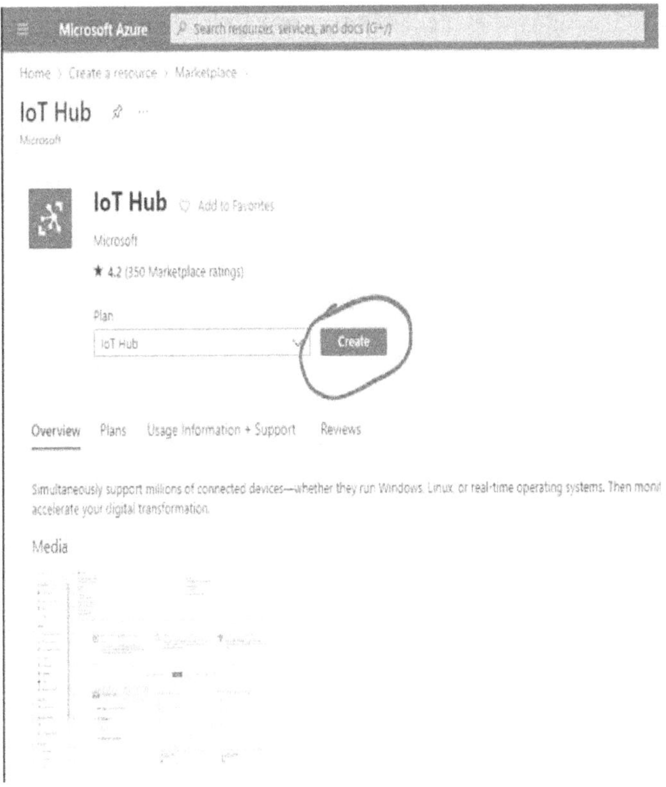

When viewing the IoT Hub Basics page, first choose a Subscription from the list.

We need to create a new resource group named after the word "picowresources." Then we need to gather our resources so we can complete this step.

Because naming our IoT Hub is the next step, we need to make sure our name is unique. The Interface will warn us if it isn't. Select a name like "picowhub1" for our Hub.

Select a region that's close to you; I've chosen "North Europe" for its recent releases.

Something similar to the following should be included:

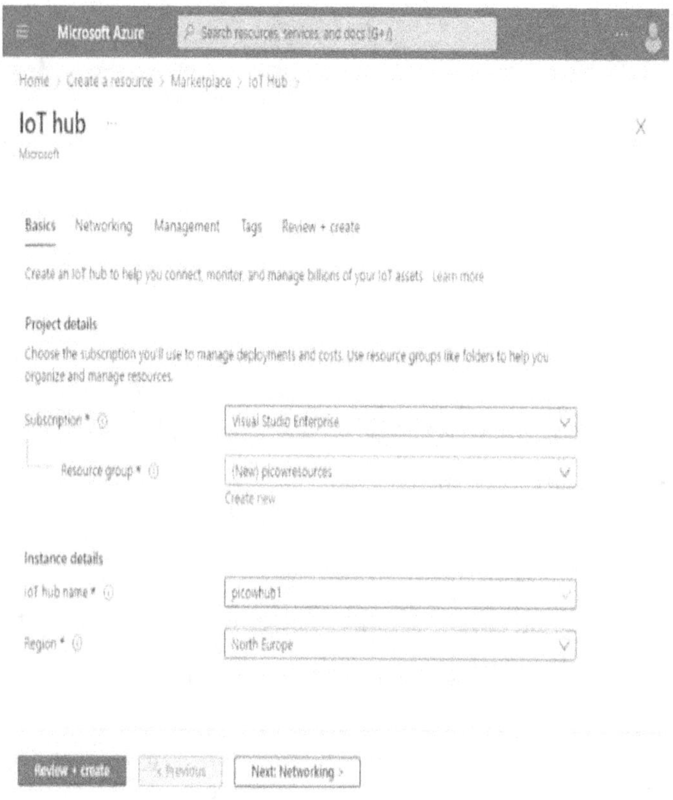

An IoT hub is a component of Azure Portal – IoT Hub. This component is the foundational layer for understanding the structure of Azure Portal – IoT Hub.

Simply press the "Next: Networking" button to bypass this page and move on to the next. A "Next: Management" button awaits nearby.

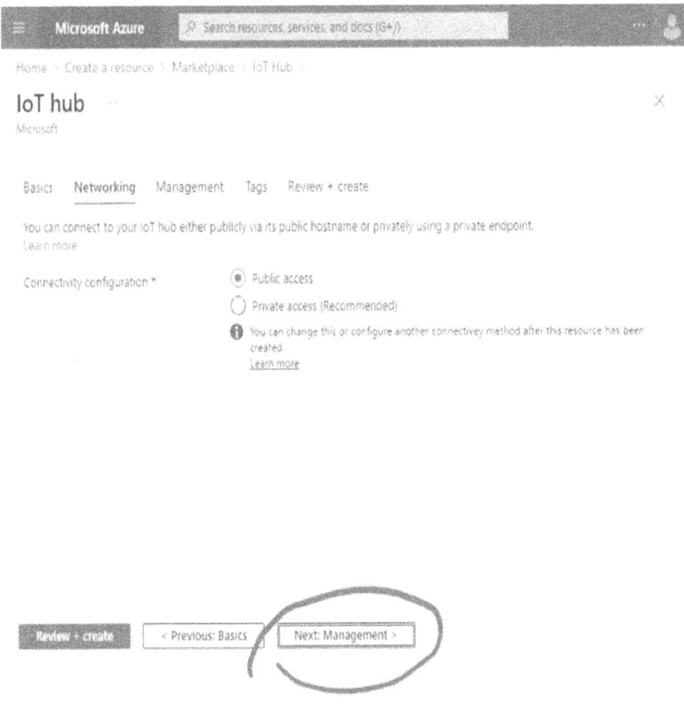

Azure Portal, an IoT Hub and networking portal, is located on the second floor.

From the drop-down menu labeled "Pricing and Scale tier," choose option F1: the Free Tier.

A single page may contain only one of these. When it's selected, a note appears informing the viewer that they've used their page.

Azure Portal manages the IoT Hub, a portal with azure tiles.

In order to review our selections and create a new tier, we must press the blue "Review + create" button in the bottom left corner of the screen. I have already chosen a Standard Tier after using up my free IoT hub.

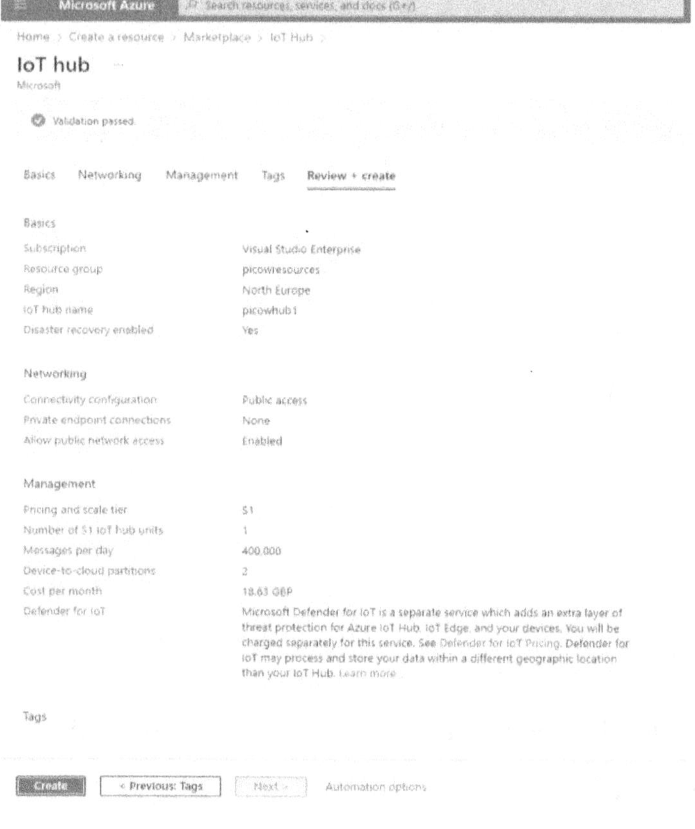

Review Azure Portal – IoT Hub and create your own.

To create your IoT Hub, press the blue "Create" button.

After the process is finished, press the blue "Go to resource" button to access the IoT Hub.

The Azure Portal — an IoT hub — was recently created.

To create an Azure IoT Hub Device, perform the following steps: a) Create an Azure IoT Hub. b) Add a Device to the IoT Hub.

We must create a device in the hub registry for our Pico W to connect and send and receive messages. This is because the IoT Hub contains an IoT Hub Device Registry.

Within the "Device Management" section of the IoT Hub's left menu, select the "Devices" option from the menu to access a page containing a list of all devices managed by the IoT Hub.

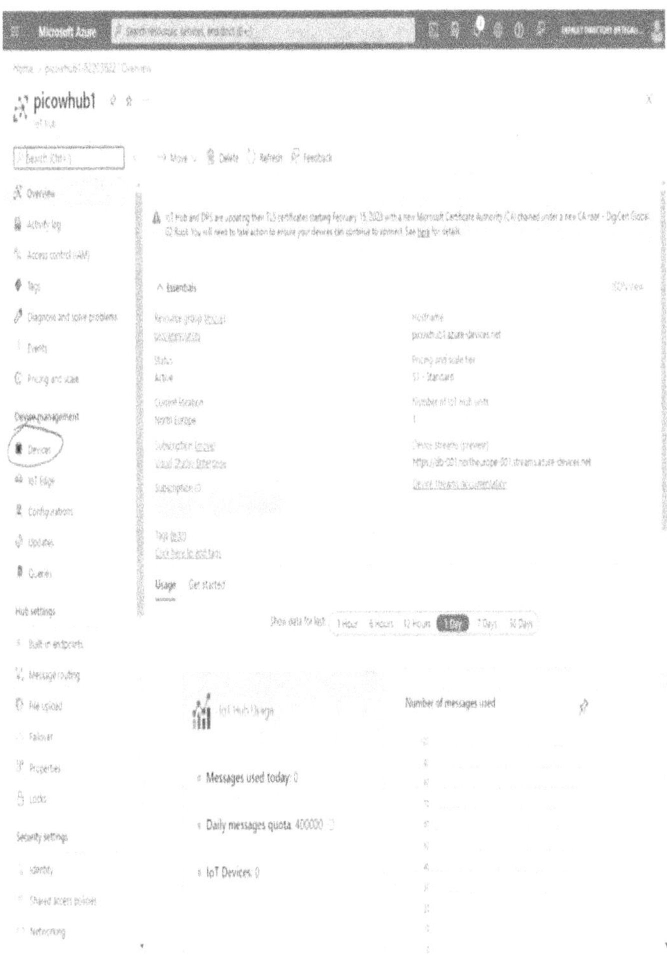

Chapter Six

The Azure Portal includes the IoT Hub, a place to access many devices.

The registry of registered devices is accessible via the IoT hub Registry > Device Registry. Called the Device Registry, this lists all registered IoT devices.

Click the Plus button to add a new device our pico-computers connect to.

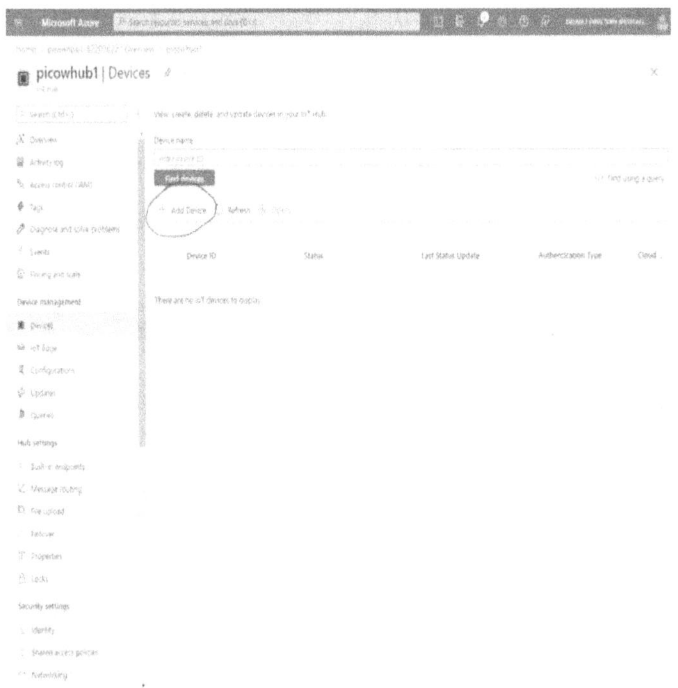

The Add Device button on the Azure Portal, IoT Hub and other devices.

I name my device on the "Create a device" page as "Picow."

When pairing a device with an IoT Hub, select the option to connect this device to an IoT Hub and set its authentication type to Symmetric Key. Copying and pasting these settings into the textbox will create a secure connection between the device and IoT Hub.

After selecting the "Save" option from the menu, press the button to create your new device.

Creating a Device page in the IoT Hub requires an original device.

After adding your new device, you'll go back to the "Devices" page. You should refresh the page if your new device isn't displayed yet.

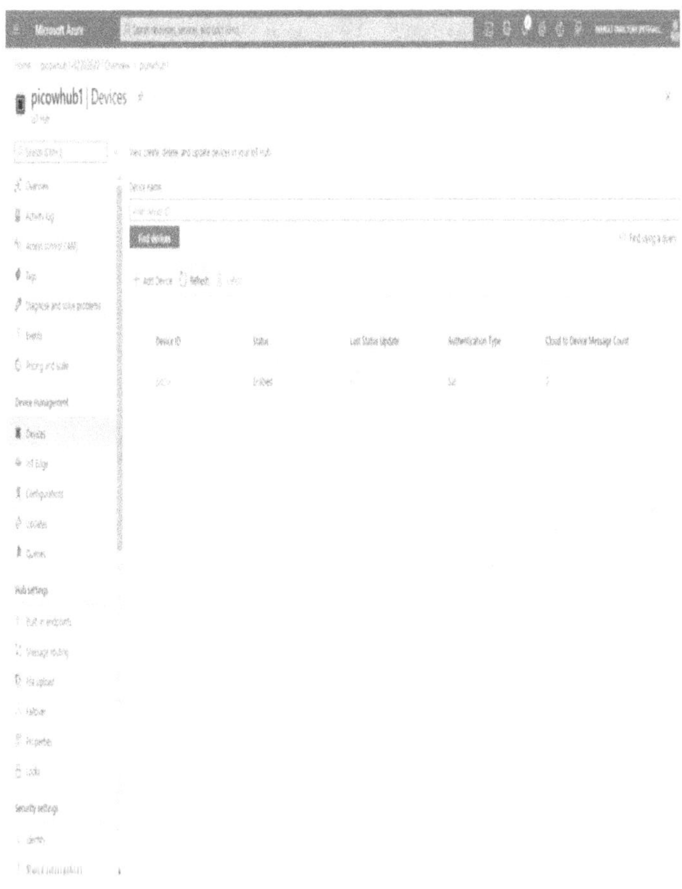

In the IoT Hub, registries are maintained for all devices.

Connecting the Azure IoT Explorer Tool completes step 5.

We'll use our Raspberry Pi Pico W to send data over to the Hub in a telemetry fashion.

To track newly sent messages, we utilize the Azure Iot Explorer tool.

This app will allow us to create relevant connection details to connect our Pico W to the IoT Hub and authenticate.

Download the release 0.14.10 of the Azure IoT Hub Explorer from GitHub. This program allows you to access the latest Azure IoT Hub files.

When you open the Azure IoT Explorer app, click the button labeled "+ Add connection" to add a new connection to our hub.

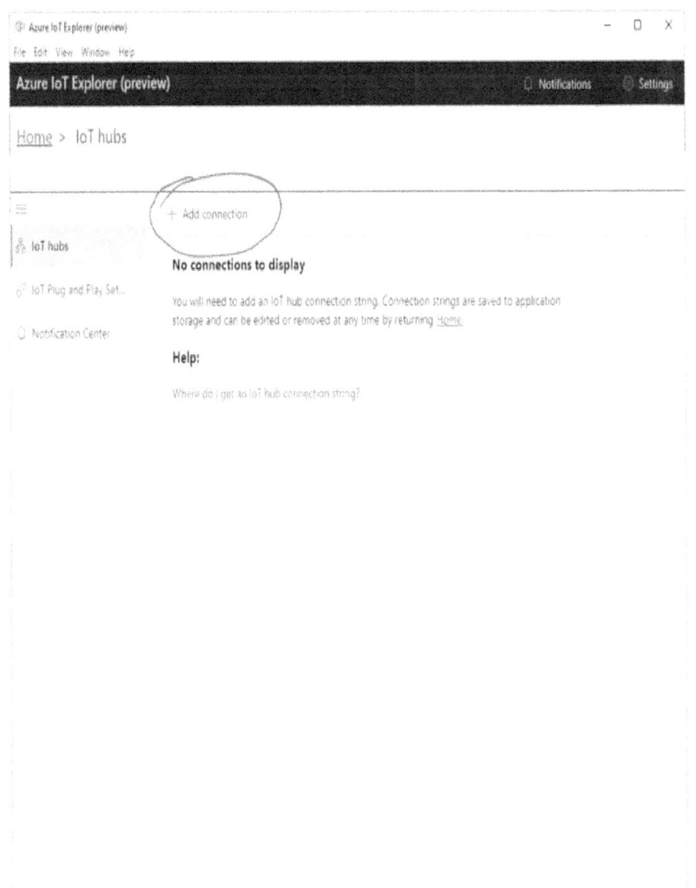

Azure IOT Explorer adds a button that connects the device to the IoT network.

In order to connect to the Azure IoT Explorer, we need to provide it with a connected string from the IoT Hub.

From the "Security Settings" menu section of the IoT Hub, click the "Shared access policies" option.

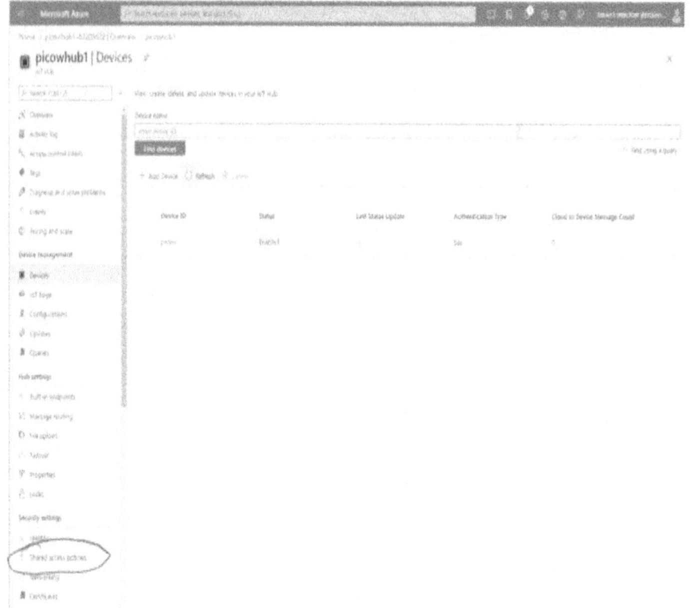

 By accessing the menu option titled "Shared Access Policies," users can access the IoT Hub's settings.

This page registers apps and services to authorize access to our IoT hub. From here, they can perform functions on the hub.

By granting apps and services specific permissions, we can limit the scope of their functionality. This is done through a Shared Access Policy.

IoT Hubs come with policies built into them. These policies are automatically generated when the hub is created.

The Explorer tool's policy is set to "iothubowner" with full access. Click the iothubowner in the list of policies to change it.

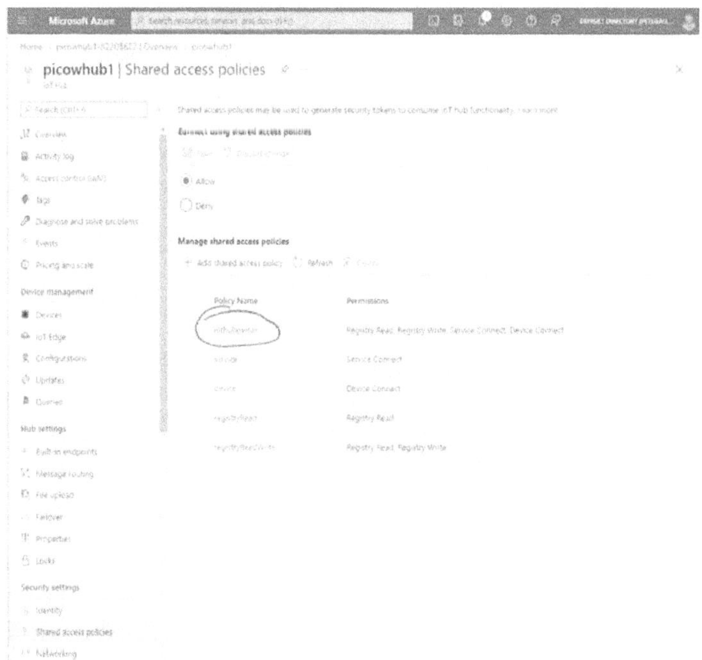

Regarding the IoT Hub, shared access policies are in effect.

Additional information regarding this regulation flyouts appears alongside it.

Next to the "Primary connection string" item, press the copy button to access it.

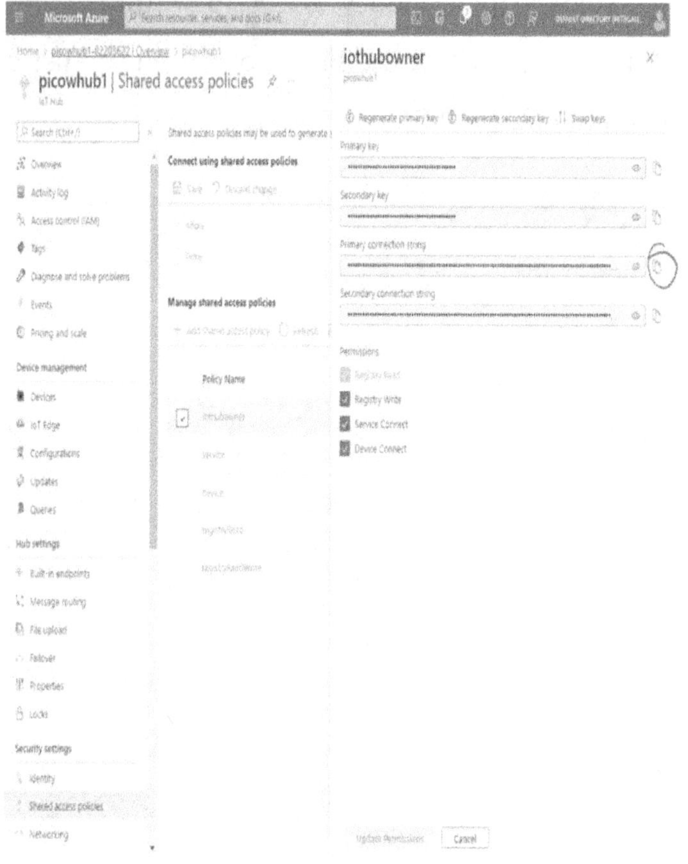

The IoT Hub — iothubowner Shared Access Policy.

After connecting to the Azure IoT Explorer, paste in the connection string and press the "Save" button.

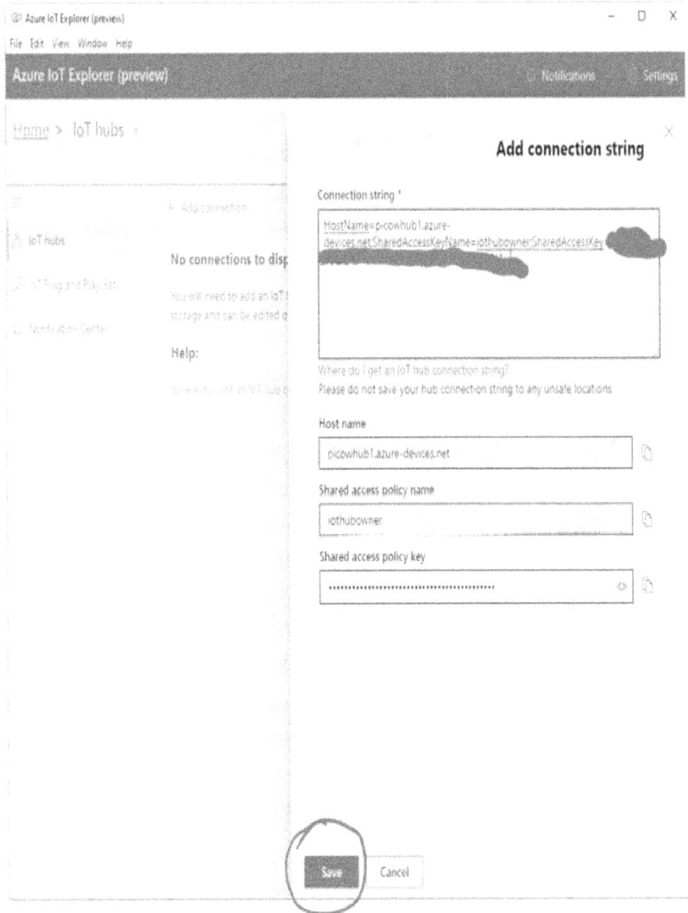

Azure IoT Explorer requires a connection string to connect to other devices.

Your device picow shows as the only device on your list.

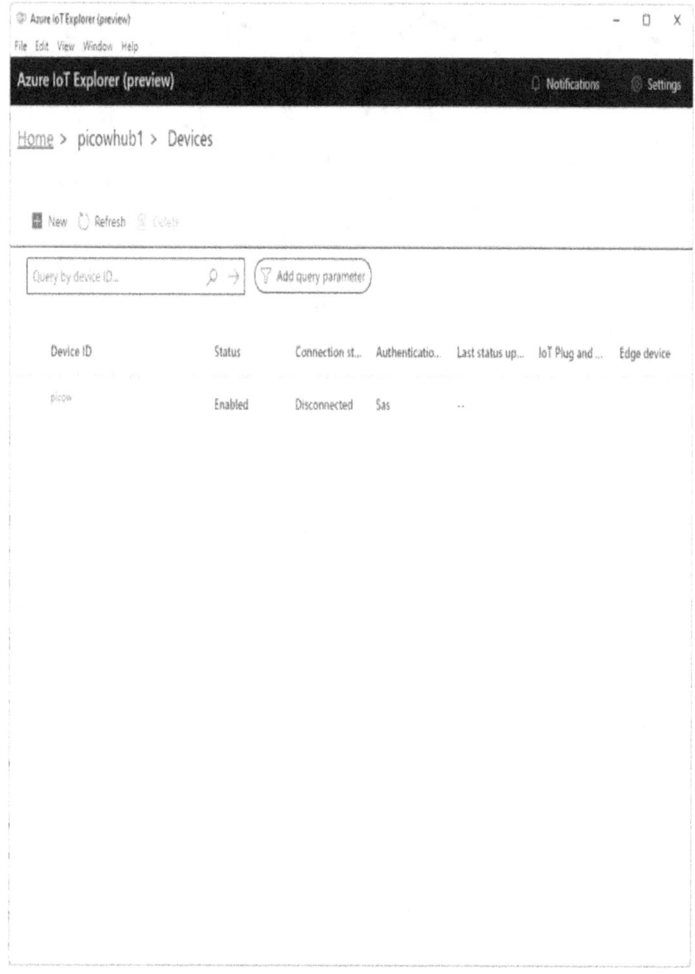

IoT Explorer on Azure provides access to devices.

Install the umqtt.simple Python package, step 6.

To communicate between the Pico W and the IoT Hub, we need to use MQTT.

We'll be using the MicroPython umqtt.simple module to achieve this.

You can easily download this Module from our Pico by choosing that option.

In the Thonny IDE, highlight the Pico W in the bottom right corner of the screen and make sure it reads "MicroPython (Raspberry Pi Pico)". You must connect your Pico W to your PC before opening the program.

Thonny IDE's Target Selection is a word puzzle that can be solved using letters and words available in the English language.

Once we enter commands into the third from the bottom section of the Shell program, the Pico W will connect to our local Wi-Fi.

Next to the last set of ">>>" brackets in the Shell, find a cursor.

Thonny's Shell Prompt can be found on her right pectoral.

We need to import the Network Module by pasting in the following line and pressing Enter.

import the network as a whole

When defining our Wi-Fi network's name, replace SSID_NAME with the name you chose.

The name of the SSID is SSID_NAME.

The new password is WIFI_PASSWORD and can be found in the replacement text.

The password is "WIFI_PASSWORD."

We can establish a Wi-Fi connection next.

To create a WLAN, call the STA_IF of the network with wlan = network.WLAN .

We can now connect to the internet via Wi-Fi.

wlan.active(True)

After connecting to Wi-Fi, we can access any services.

Connect to the wireless network with the specified ssid and password.

Once we connect to the Wi-Fi network, we can download the umqtt.simple MicroPython module.

To properly utilize this module, we need to import the package upip.

import Upip

To add the umqtt.simple module, we need to manually install it.

upip.install('umqtt.simple')

A prompt should appear stating "Installing to: /lib/" followed by a warning about the SSL certificate. The message should then state that the package is installing Umqtt.simple.

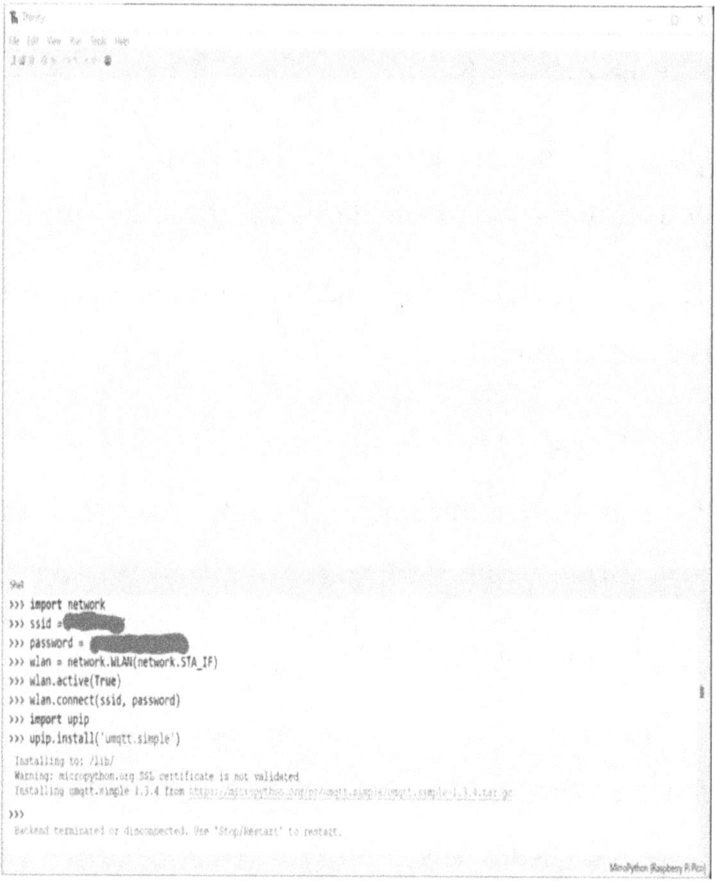

Shell

```
>>> import network
>>> ssid =
>>> password =
>>> wlan = network.WLAN(network.STA_IF)
>>> wlan.active(True)
>>> wlan.connect(ssid, password)
>>> import upip
>>> upip.install('umqtt.simple')
 Installing to: /lib/
 Warning: micropython.org SSL certificate is not validated
 Installing umqtt.simple 1.3.4 from https://micropython.org/pi/umqtt.simple/umqtt.simple-1.3.4.tar.gz
>>>
 Backend terminated or disconnected. Use 'Stop/Restart' to restart.
```

MicroPython (Raspberry Pi Pico)

Thonny used umqtt.simplete to complete the installation.

You must press the "Stop/Restart" button in the toolbar to reconnect to the Pico W.

The Azure IoT Hub MQTT Code needs to be entered on Step 7.

Copy and paste the following text into a new file.

```python
import network
import time
import machine

from umqtt.simple import MQTTClient
from machine import Pin

ssid = 'SSID_NAME'
password = 'WIFI_PASSWORD'

wlan = network.WLAN(network.STA_IF)
wlan.active(True)
```

```python
wlan.connect(ssid, password)

# Wait for connect or fail
max_wait = 10
while max_wait > 0:
    if wlan.status() < 0 or wlan.status() >= 3:
        break
    max_wait -= 1
    print('waiting for connection...')
    time.sleep(1)

# Handle connection error
if wlan.status() != 3:
    raise RuntimeError('network connection failed')
else:
    print('connected')
    status = wlan.ifconfig()
    print( 'ip = ' + status[0] )

led = Pin(15, Pin.OUT)
button = Pin(14, Pin.IN, Pin.PULL_DOWN)

hostname = 'YOUR_IOT_HUB_NAME.azure-devices.net'
clientid = 'picow'
user_name = 'YOUR_IOT_HUB_NAME.azure-devices.net/picow/?api-version=2021-04-
12'
passw = 'YOUR_SAS_TOKEN'
topic_pub = b'devices/picow/messages/events/'
topic_msg = b'{"buttonpressed":"1"}'
port_no = 0
subscribe_topic = "devices/picow/messages/devicebound/#"

def mqtt_connect():
```

```python
    certificate_path = "baltimore.cer"
    print('Loading Blatimore Certificate')
    with open(certificate_path, 'r') as f:
        cert = f.read()
    print('Obtained Baltimore Certificate')
    sslparams = {'cert':cert}

    client = MQTTClient(client_id=clientid, server=hostname, port=port_no,
user=user_name, password=passw, keepalive=3600, ssl=True,
ssl_params=sslparams)
    client.connect()
    print('Connected to IoT Hub MQTT Broker')
    return client

def reconnect():
    print('Failed to connect to the MQTT Broker. Reconnecting...')
    time.sleep(5)
    machine.reset()

def callback_handler(topic, message_receive):
    print("Received message")
    print(message_receive)
    if message_receive.strip() == b'led_on':
```

```python
            led.value(1)
        else:
            led.value(0)

    try:
        client = mqtt_connect()
        client.set_callback(callback_handler)
        client.subscribe(topic=subscribe_topic)
    except OSError as e:
        reconnect()

    while True:

        client.check_msg()

        if button.value():
            client.publish(topic_pub, topic_msg)
            time.sleep(0.5)
        else:
            pass
```

Code explanations provide further insight into the meaning of the code.

Module Imports provides access to additional modules.

This includes importing the necessary supporting modules at the beginning of the code.

```
import network
import time
import machine

from umqtt.simple import MQTTClient
from machine import Pin
```

We interact with the Pico W GPIO through a machine and the "network" for our Wi-Fi connection. Additionally, we rely on time to account for any delays.

We include the "MQTTClient" from the "umqtt.simple" module as well.

Easily connect to the internet through Wi-Fi.

Connect to the internet via Wi-Fi.

```python
ssid = 'SSID_NAME'
password = 'WIFI_PASSWORD'

wlan = network.WLAN(network.STA_IF)
wlan.active(True)
wlan.connect(ssid, password)

# Wait for connect or fail
max_wait = 10




while max_wait > 0:
    if wlan.status() < 0 or wlan.status() >= 3:
        break
    max_wait -= 1
    print('waiting for connection...')
    time.sleep(1)

# Handle connection error
if wlan.status() != 3:
    raise RuntimeError('network connection failed')
else:
    print('connected')
    status = wlan.ifconfig()
    print( 'ip = ' + status[0] )
```

In the next section, you need to replace two placeholder variables with new ones first.

Once we've established a connection via Wi-Fi, we wait for the connection to finish.

Chapter Seven

GPIO Setup

In order to properly set up GPIO inputs and outputs, we need to first create them.

led = Pin(15, Pin.OUT)

button = Pin(14, Pin.IN, Pin.PULL_DOWN)

We pull Pin 14 down to use as an input for our button; we set Pin 15 to be an output for our LED.

MQTT Variables

Provides a more flexible alternative to standard text variables.

We set up variables for our various MQTT settings by choosing from a list.

```python
hostname = 'YOUR_IOT_HUB_NAME.azure-devices.net'
clientid = 'picow'
user_name = 'YOUR_IOT_HUB_NAME.azure-devices.net/picow/?api-version=2021-04-12'
passw = 'YOUR_SAS_TOKEN'
topic_pub = b'devices/picow/messages/events/'
topic_msg = b'{"buttonpressed":"1"}'
port_no = 0
subscribe_topic = "devices/picow/messages/devicebound/#"
```

Next, we need to fill in the placeholders along this section. These are listed after the original text.

This information uses the following MQTT variables:

Variable	Usage
hostname	The public endpoint for our IoT hub
clientid	The Device ID for the IoT Hub Device
user_name	Part of the authentication for connection to the IoT Hub
passw	A generated SAS token for authentication to the IoT Hub
topic_pub	The MQTT topic under wihch to publish our telemetry messages
topic_msg	The MQTT Message we'll be sending to the IoT Hub
port_no	The port number we'll be using to communicate over MQTT to the IoT Hub. 0 will use the default MQTT port, in our case 8883 as we're using SSL
subscribe_topic	The MQTT Topic which allows us to receive IoT Hub to Device (Cloud-to-device) messages

It includes a MQTT Connect capability.

We establish a regular procedure to connect to the MQTT IoT Hub Broker.

```python
def mqtt_connect():

    certificate_path = "baltimore.cer"
    print('Loading Blatimore Certificate')
    with open(certificate_path, 'r') as f:
        cert = f.read()
    print('Obtained Baltimore Certificate')
    sslparams = {'cert':cert}

    client = MQTTClient(client_id=clientid, server=hostname, port=port_no,
user=user_name, password=passw, keepalive=3600, ssl=True,
ssl_params=sslparams)
    client.connect()
    print('Connected to IoT Hub MQTT Broker')
    return client
```

Step 9, add the Baltimore SSL certificate from Pico W's storage to our copy.

This certificate allows us to securely connect to the IoT Hub over SSL. It encrypts our telemetry traffic.

To create our MQTT client, we pass in the Client ID, Server, Port number, User Name, Password, Keep Alive Time, SSL Switch and SSL Parameters.

We connect to the IoT Hub MQTT channel, which we use to access our MQTT client for future uses throughout the program.

A description of the MQTT reconnect procedure is provided below.

We establish MQTT Reconnect Routines that we named after the original routine.

```
def reconnect():
    print('Failed to connect to the MQTT Broker. Reconnecting...')
    time.sleep(5)
    machine.reset()
```

When we can't connect to the IoT Hub or lose our MQTT connection, we lose control of the Pico W for a brief time. This causes us to lose connection to

Thonny. As a result, we need to use the "Stop and Reset" button to re-run our code with F5.

The MQTT InTouch Hub to Pico W (Cloud to Device) Message Handler Procedure

This allows messages from the cloud to be associated with device functionality. Because the IoT Hub sends messages to the Device, we can process that event.

```python
def callback_handler(topic, message_receive):
    print("Received message")
    print(message_receive)
    if message_receive.strip() == b'led on':
        led.value(1)
    else:
        led.value(0)
```

The IoT Hub sends messages from the cloud to devices known as "Cloud-to-Device" messaging. We can handle these messages.

Next, we'll connect this function to the program.

We show the contents of the message received from the hub along with any relevant printing.

If we determine the message indicates we should turn the LED on, we do that.

The .strip() string function removes any blank spaces from our message.

When comparing the message to the IoT Hub, we convert the Byte Literal that stores our "led_on" string to match the Hub's Message.

Subscribe to messages sent between devices and their IoT Hub MQTT connections.

Once everything is in place, we can connect to the IoT Hub MQTT Broker with no issues.

```
try:
    client = mqtt_connect()
    client.set_callback(callback_handler)
    client.subscribe(topic=subscribe_topic)
except OSError as e:
    reconnect()
```

MQTT is a protocol used to transfer information between machines. Before we can use it, we need to connect to the MQTT Hub via our "mqtt_connect" function.

We determine how we process incoming messages from our IoT Hub using a specific procedure.

The IoT hub delivers messages via the Pico W about the subject it's about.

We check for a connection failure before attempting to reconnect. Doing so via a process known as reconnectation.

The Main Program Loop

The final section of our programming code is the main program loop.

```
client.check_msg()

if button.value():
    client.publish(topic_pub, topic_msg)
    time.sleep(0.5)
else:
    pass
```

While looping infinitely in the last section of our code, we stated the statement "while True" .

We use the "client.check_msg()" procedure to check for any messages received through our IoT hub.

We need to check for a button press when we receive a message. That's why we need a wait call. We can also use the call for messaging.

This block of code ensures the current value of our button.

When the button is pressed, we publish a MQTT message with the Topic we defined in our MQTT variables and a message reflecting that the button has been pressed.

Before moving on, we pause for half a second.

Bypassing the pass keyword in an if statement is an unnecessary action.

Replace the placeholder text in Step 8.

To properly connect to Wi-Fi, you need to adjust the "ssid" and "password" variables in this code. Change them to the name of your network and password.

Next, change the name of your IoT Hub to match what you named it. In my case, this was the name of my IoT Hub, which was "picowhub1". Once changed, my hostname variable becomes 'picowhub1.azure-devices.net'.

We need the SAS Token to connect with the Hub; next we'll need to acquire it.

To produce this token, we need to use the Azure IoT Explorer software we installed in Step 5.

On the "Device identity" page for our device, we can find the Device ID and Connections Strings, as well as Primary and Secondary Keys. Clicking on the "picow" icon in the devices list brings us to this page.

To the right of this, we have a section titled "Connecting string with SAS token" that reveals additional content when clicked. This area allows us to define and create our SAS token.

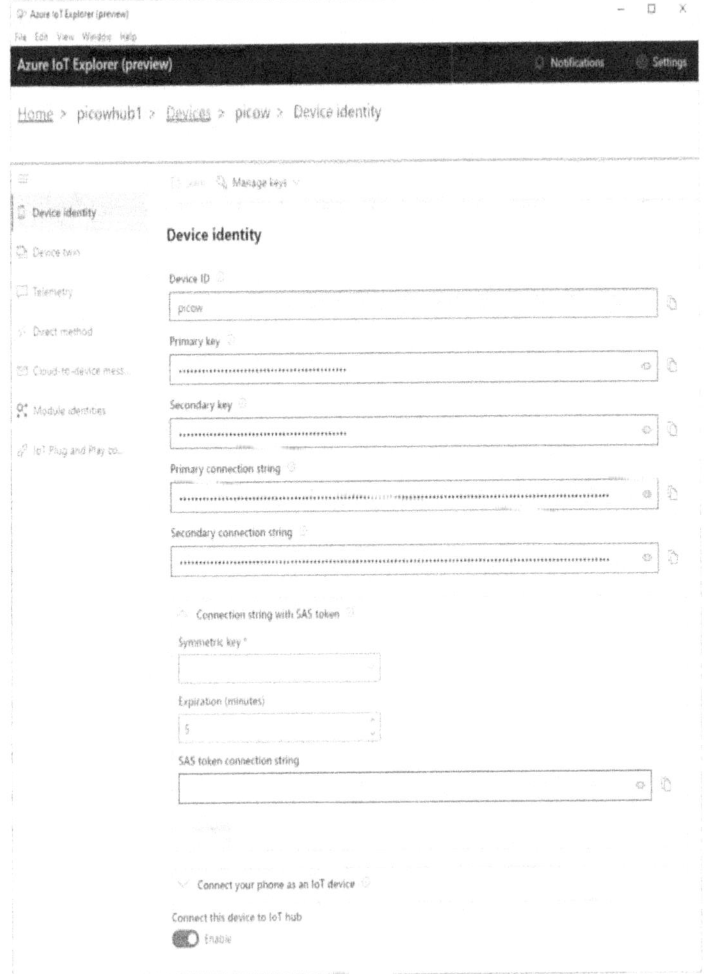

Azure IoT Explorer generates a SAS token from the data it collects.

Select "Symmetric key" from the drop-down menu, then choose "Primary key" from the list. In the box labeled "Expiration time," decrease the number five by one and then hit the generate button.

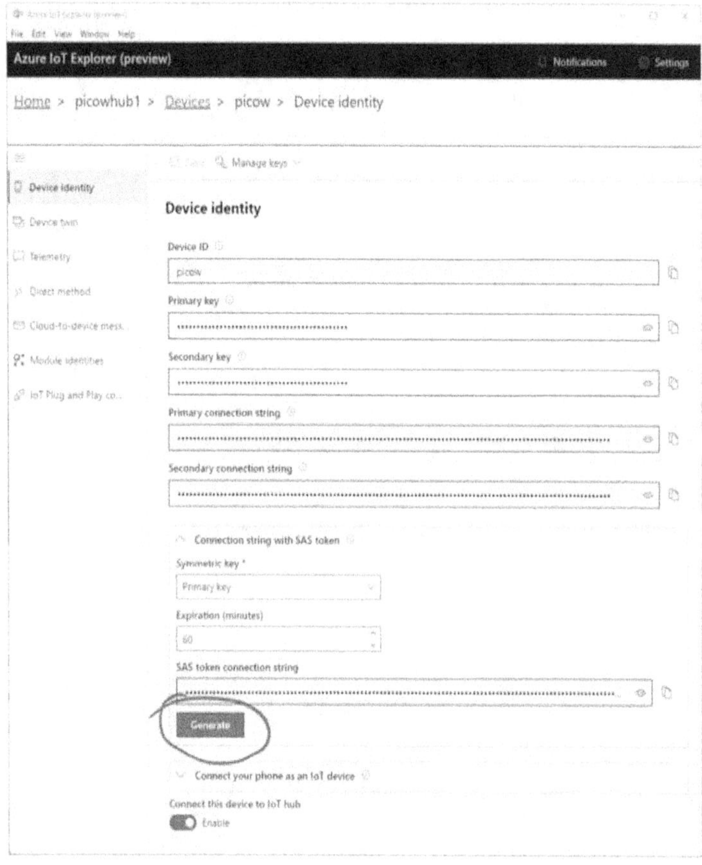

Azure IoT Explorer provided a SAS token as its output.

To the right of the "SAS token connection string" box, pressing the copy button will copy the SAS Token.

My SAS Token resembles the following image as redactions have been applied to the actual object.

```
HostName=picowhub1.azure-
devices.net;DeviceId=picow;SharedAccessSignature=SharedAccessSignature
sr=picowhub1.azure-
devices.net%2Fdevices%2Fpicow&sig=<redacted>%3D&se=1659481856
```

By replacing the "YOUR_SAS_TOKEN" placeholder for the "passw" variable with our SAS Token, we can connect to our SAS. However, this connection string needs some alterations. Remove the line that contains "HostName" and "DeviceId," along with the line that contains "SharedAccessSignature=." Additionally, remove the word "YOUR_SAS_TOKEN" from the placeholders line.

Your SAS token variable definition should look like this once the update finishes.

```
passw = 'SharedAccessSignature sr=picowhub1.azure-
devices.net%2Fdevices%2Fpicow&sig=<redacted>%3D&se=1659481856'
```

Confirm SharedAccessSignature is supposed to be separated from sr= by a gap.

Rename the file to "iothub1.py" and then save it to the Raspberry Pi.

9. Adding the Baltimore Certificate

Our MQTT connection to the Azure IoT Hub requires using the Baltimore SSL certificate to secure the communication.

Step 10: Sending Telemetry to the IoT Hub

This document already appears in the code, we need to add it to the Pico W project as well.

Paste the following text into a new file.

```
-----BEGIN CERTIFICATE-----
MIIDdzCCAl+gAwIBAgIEAgAAuTANBgkqhkiG9w0BAQUFADBaMQswCQYDVQQGEwJJ
RTESMBAGA1UEChMJQmFsdGltb3JlMRMwEQYDVQQLEwpDeWJlclRydXN0MSIwIAYD
VQQDExlCYWx0aW1vcmUgQ3liZXJUcnVzdCBSb290MB4XDTAwMDUxMjE4NDYwMFoX
DTI1MDUxMjIzNTkwMFowWjELMAkGA1UEBhMCSUUxEjAQBgNVBAoTCUJhbHRpbW9y
ZTETMBEGA1UECxMKQ3liZXJUcnVzdDEiMCAGA1UEAxMZQmFsdGltb3JlIEN5YmVy
VHJ1c3QgUm9vdDCCASIwDQYJKoZIhvcNAQEBBQADggEPADCCAQoCggEBAKMEuyKr
mD1X6CZymrV51Cni4eiVgLGw41uOKymaZN+hXe2wCQVt2yguzmKiYv60iNoS6zjr
IZ3AQSsBUnuId9Mcj8e6uYi1agnnc+gRQKfRzMpijS3ljwumUNKoUMMo6vWrJYeK
mpYcqWe4PwzV9/1SEy/CG9VwcPCPwBLKBsua4dnKM3p31vjsufFoREJIE9LAwqSu
XmD+tqYF/LTdB1kC1FkYmGP1pWPgkAx9XbIGevOF6uvUA65ehD5f/xXtabz5OTZy
dc93Uk3zyZAsuT31ySNTPx8kmCFcB5kpvcY67Oduhjpr13RjM71oGDHweI12v/ye
jl0qhqdNkNwnGjkCAwEAAaNFMEMwHQYDVR0OBBYEFOWdWTCCR1jMrPoIVDaGezq1
BE3wMBIGA1UdEwEB/wQIMAYBAf8CAQMwDgYDVR0PAQH/BAQDAgEGMA0GCSqGSIb3
DQEBBQUAA4IBAQCFDF2O5G9RaEIFoN27Tyc1hAO992T9Ldcw46QQF+vaKSm2eT92
9hkTI7gQCv1YpNRhcL0EYWoSihfVCr3FvDB81ukMJY2GQE/szKN+OMY3EU/t3Wgx
jkzSswF07r51XqdIGn9w/xZchMB5hbqF/X++ZRGjD8ACtPhSNzkE1akxehi/oCr0
Epn3o0WC4zxe9Z2etciefC7IpJ5OCBRLbf1wbWsaY71k5h+3zvDyny67G7fyUIhz
ksLi4xaNmjICq44Y3ekQEe5+NauQrz4wlHrQMz2nZQ/1/I6eYs9HRCwBXbsdtTLS
R9I4LtD+gdwyah617jzV/OeBHRnDJELqYzmp
-----END CERTIFICATE-----
```

The file needs to be transferred to the Raspberry Pi as "baltimore.cer," with the intention that it be directed at the Pico.

Sending telemetry to the IoT Hub at the end of Step 10.

We can now run our code and check that the Pico W connects to the Wi-Fi and then our smart hub.

Press the green "Run current script" button in the toolbar to run the current code. Alternatively, press F5 to run the button's code.

When connected to Wi-Fi, the Pico W prints its assigned IP address.

Once connected to the IoT Hub, the Baltimore Certificate should be loaded.

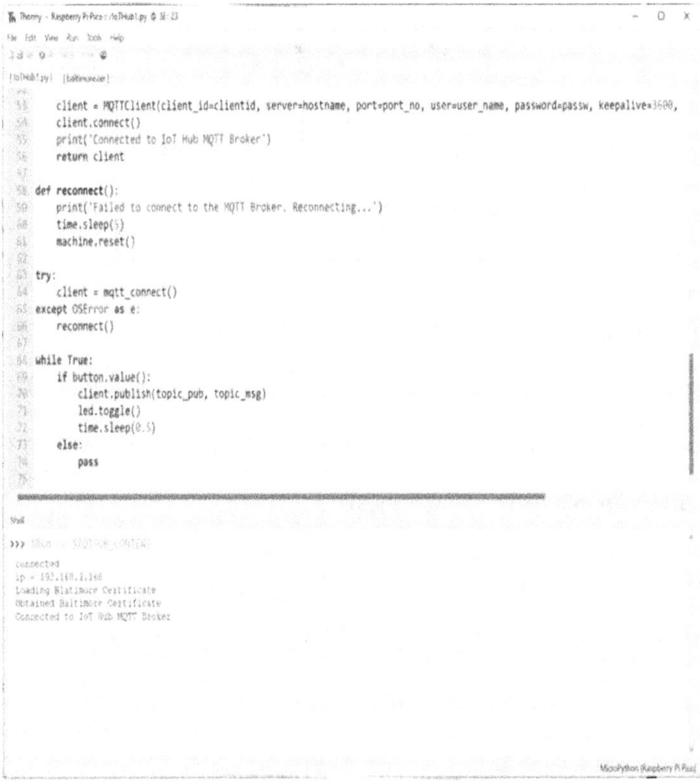

```python
    client = MQTTClient(client_id=clientid, server=hostname, port=port_no, user=user_name, password=passw, keepalive=3600,
    client.connect()
    print('Connected to IoT Hub MQTT Broker')
    return client

def reconnect():
    print('Failed to connect to the MQTT Broker. Reconnecting...')
    time.sleep(5)
    machine.reset()

try:
    client = mqtt_connect()
except OSError as e:
    reconnect()

while True:
    if button.value():
        client.publish(topic_pub, topic_msg)
        led.toggle()
        time.sleep(0.5)
    else:
        pass
```

```
>>> %Run -c $EDITOR_CONTENT

connected
ip = 192.168.1.168
Loading Baltimore Certificate
Obtained Baltimore Certificate
Connected to IoT Hub MQTT Broker
```

Chapter Eight

Thonny's IoT Hub code is running.

A likely cause of the error "MQTTException: 5" is that the SAS token has expired. To solve this problem, regenerate a new token and then paste it over the expired one. Add nine zeroes to the front of the new code and run the code again.

Make sure you configure the IoT Hub correctly and haven't mistyped its name. If that doesn't work, make sure all variables are configured correctly.

We need to switch to the Azure IoT Explorer when we need to monitor our telemetry data that we send with it.

On the menu on the far left, click the "Telemetry" option.

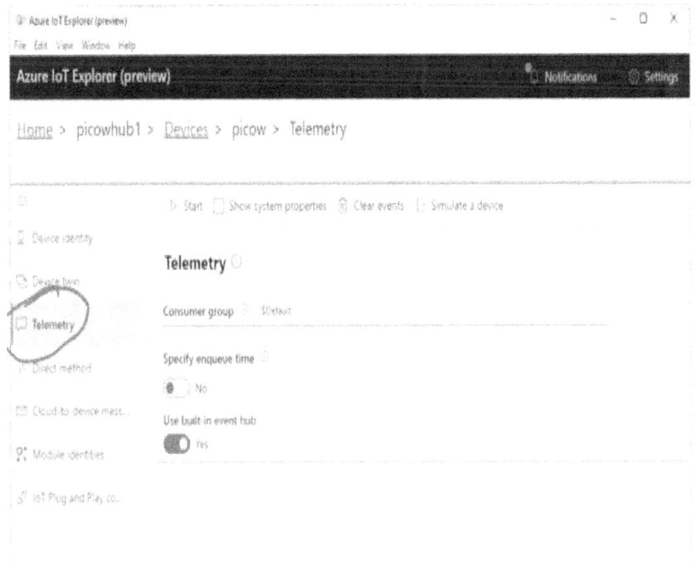

Azure IoT Explorer provides insight into the device's health and status through telemetry.

By pressing the "Start" button in the toolbar at the top of our dashboard, we can begin monitoring the data we send.

You should be able to press the button on our wood board, which prompts the message to appear in the Azure IoT Explorer Telemetry window.

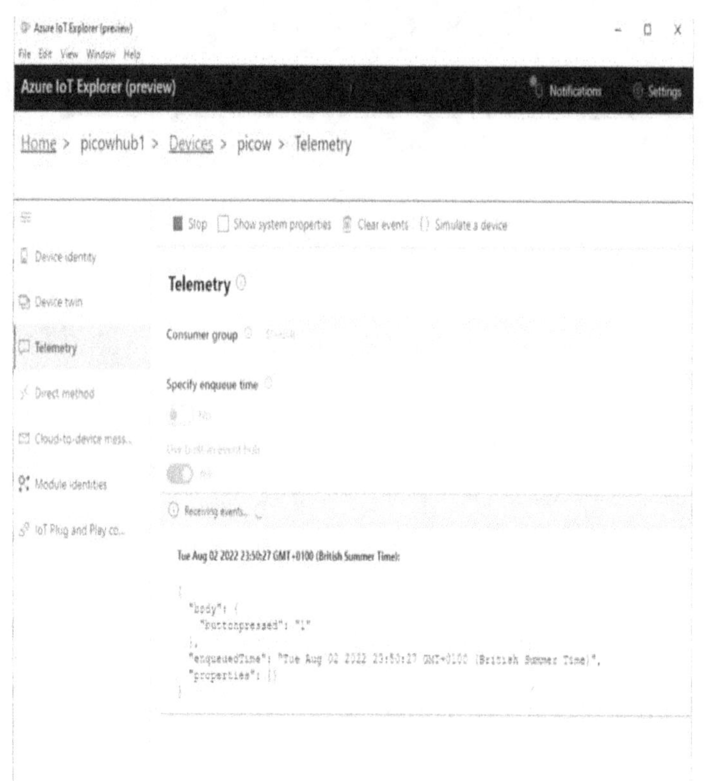

Azure IoT Explorer displays telemetry received messages.

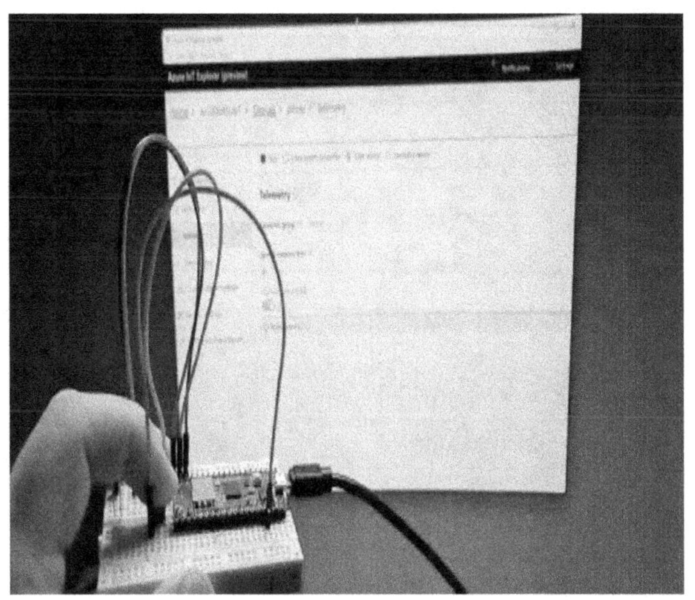

To receive cloud to device messages, perform step 11.

We can now broadcast MQTT messages from the IoT hub to other devices over Pico W.

To end the Azure IoT Explorer's telemetry monitoring, press the "Stop" button in its toolbar.

To access this feature, press the icon marked "Cloud-to-device message" on the menu on the left. A page showing this function appears.

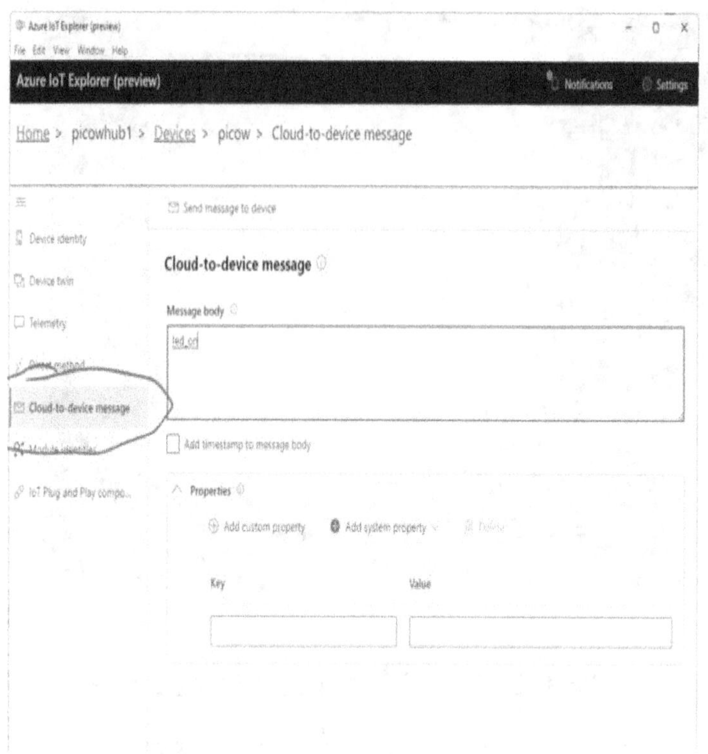

Messages from the Azure IoT Explorer go from the cloud to the device.

Click the toolbar's "Send message to device" button to input the phrase "led_on" in the text box.

Your LED should now shine.

The LED lights up when a cloud-to-device message is received.

When sent to a device with a "led_off" setting, pressing the "Send message to device" button again turns its LED off.

To finish a piece of writing with an abstract statement.

The Azure IoT Hub obtains two-way communication with the Pico W.

Use any of the services at your disposal when processing telemetry from the Pico W sensors connected to it. This is from where you can start.

The IoT Hub can issue commands to the Pico to perform tasks.

www.ingramcontent.com/pod-product-compliance
Lightning Source LLC
Chambersburg PA
CBHW071528150726
48000CB00002B/724